FA

REASON,

AND

THE WAR

AGAINST

JIHADISM

Tranquillitas Ordinis: *The Present Failure and
Future Promise of American Catholic Thought
on War and Peace*

Catholicism and the Renewal of American Democracy

*American Interests, American Purpose:
Moral Reasoning and U.S. Foreign Policy*

*Freedom and Its Discontents:
Catholicism Confronts Modernity*

Just War and the Gulf War
(with James Turner Johnson)

*The Final Revolution: The Resistance Church
and the Collapse of Communism*

*Soul of the World: Notes on the Future
of Public Catholicism*

Witness to Hope: The Biography of Pope John Paul II

The Truth of Catholicism: Ten Controversies Explored

*The Courage to Be Catholic: Crisis, Reform,
and the Future of the Church*

Letters to a Young Catholic

*The Cube and the Cathedral: Europe, America,
and Politics Without God*

*God's Choice: Pope Benedict XVI and the Future
of the Catholic Church*

FAITH, REASON, AND THE WAR AGAINST JIHADISM

GEORGE WEIGEL

Image Books/Doubleday Religion
New York London Toronto Sydney Auckland

IMAGE, the Image colophon, and DOUBLEDAY are
registered trademarks of Random House, Inc.

Originally published in hardcover in the
United States in slightly different form by
Doubleday in 2007.

Library of Congress Cataloging-in-Publication Data
Weigel, George, 1951–
Faith, reason, and the war against jihadism / by
George Weigel.
1. Terrorism–Religious aspects. 2. Jihad. 3. War–
Religious aspects. 4. International relations. I. Title.

BL65.T47W45 2007
320.5'57–dc22
2007019211

ISBN 978-0-385-52478-0

PRINTED IN THE UNITED STATES OF AMERICA

1   3   5   7   9   10   8   6   4   2

First Paperback Edition

FOR

GEORGE CARDINAL PELL

Contents

FAITH,

REASON,

AND

THE WAR

AGAINST

JIHADISM

DEADLY
SERIOUS
BUSINESS

In October 1996, one of America's marquee corporations invited me to brief some of its promising young executives on likely "global futures."

According to the invitation, I was to stress issues and actors that weren't yet making the headlines but were likely to do so in the next decade. I made three broad points—that history can't be read exclusively through the lenses of politics, economics, or technology; that ideas have profound consequences on the dynamics of history; and that the vitality and morale of one's culture (which include a sense of its future possibilities) are the keys to civilizational success and influence over the long haul. Among the examples I used to illustrate these points: the probable rise of a resurgent Islam as a major factor in shaping the twenty-first-century world.

I was not invited back for a 1997 briefing.

Less than five years after I spoke with these young executives, a stateless man, of whom none of them had likely ever heard back in 1996, sat in a cave in the mountains of Afghanistan. He was surrounded by a few disciples, a satellite dish receiver, and a television set—the dish and the television being the products of societies the stateless man and his followers despised. The TV wasn't working very well, so one of the disciples turned on a radio and sought the BBC's Arabic service. There, he learned that an airplane had plowed into the World Trade Center in New York. He excitedly told the others, who broke into celebration; but their leader said, simply, "Wait, wait." News soon came of the second tower being hit. The leader wept, prayed—and then Osama bin Laden stunned his disciples by holding up three fingers. When they heard reports of the Pentagon being struck, bin Laden held up four fingers, amazing his followers even more. As things turned out, they would be disappointed, at least in this instance. Because of the heroic actions of the passengers on United Airlines Flight 93, who acted like free citizens rather than helpless victims, al-Qaeda's fourth target that day, the U.S. Capitol, was spared. Yet in the space of two hours, the landscape of twenty-first-century public life had been violently and radically changed.[1]

Viewed through history's wide-angle lens, the events of September 11, 2001, were one lethal expression of the fact that, contrary to secularization theory and the widespread assumptions of the world's elites (including its governmental elites), the twenty-first century will be one in which rapidly advancing modernization coincides with an explosion of religious conviction and passion. Indeed, a case can be made that the acids and volatilities of modernization have themselves contributed mightily to this remarkable global religious revival, which includes such socially and politically benign phenomena as the dramatic expansion of Pentecostalism (the fastest-growing religious phenomenon in human history) and Mormonism (the most important new religion in fourteen centuries). Yet 9/11 was, clearly, something else, and something more. For the expression of globalized religious passion Americans saw that day represented a specific and mortal threat to the civilization of the West, and to the United States as the lead society of the West. War had been declared upon us by an enemy the overwhelming majority of us did not recognize—an enemy whose motivations were utterly alien to twenty-first-century western sensibilities.

That it has taken some time for this new and dominant fact of international public life to be understood for what it is should not have been a surprise. It was difficult to recognize for what it was before it struck New York and Washington. As Lawrence Wright puts it in *The Looming Tower*, even the most acute intelligence operative, studying shards and fragments of information about al-Qaeda and its allies before 9/11, was in a position akin to that of a medical researcher looking at "a laboratory slide of some previously unseen virus."[2] Throughout the fall of 2001, comparisons were frequently made between 9/11 and another infamous date: December 7, 1941, the day Japan attacked Pearl Harbor. The analogy finally failed, however: the U.S. Navy had war-gamed a struggle with Japan for decades, and on occasion the "game" of "Blue vs. Orange" began with a surprise "Orange" strike on the U.S. Pacific Fleet at its Hawaiian anchorage. Moreover, Pearl Harbor marked the beginning of a conventional struggle between great powers; and in that sense, despite the disparity of resources between them, the war that Pearl Harbor triggered between the United States and Japan was "symmetrical." By contrast, 9/11 was the most lethal incarnation yet of "asymmetrical warfare," launched upon us by an enemy that was not a state, for reasons that far transcended conventional purposes of statecraft or *raison d'état*. And this, too, made the new circumstances in which we found ourselves hard to understand.

Other factors have contributed to the difficulty America has had in correctly identifying, and then understanding, the enemy in this new kind of war. Terrorism has a lengthy pedigree. As one of its closest students, Walter Laqueur, has pointed out, however, the terrorism practiced by the nineteenth-century anarchists who assassinated European nobility, or by the late-twentieth-century airplane hijackers of the Baader-Meinhof Gang or Black September, had propaganda as its essential purpose: these terrorists sought publicity for a specific political cause, like democracy in czarist Russia or an independent Palestinian state. The kind of terrorism visited upon America on 9/11, Laqueur argues, was different in kind, not simply in degree: this was terrorism intended to "effect maximum destruction," both material and psychological—terrorism that, as a matter of principle, declined to discriminate between those who were "guilty" (in terms of specific political grievances) and those who were "innocent" in respect to those grievances. The notion that there are "no innocents"—that the enemy is "guilty" simply by reason of drawing breath—was itself something new and reflected a deliberate strategic choice: a strategy of open-ended mayhem based on the radical dehumanization of the "other."[5]

The new kind of war that burst upon us on a clear, late-summer morning was also hard to comprehend because it did not seem to have a locus, a source point from which the attack had been launched and which could be conquered in turn, in order to remove the threat. There was no Imperial Palace as in World War II Tokyo, no Chancellery as there had been in Hitler's Berlin, to provide a symbolic geographic reference point for our war effort. There wasn't even something like the old Comintern, a Cold War agency of subversion, internationally networked

but run from Moscow Center. Rather, we were confronted by disparate groups, none of them traditional
state "actors" in the great game of international politics, bound together, not by conventional political
bonds, but by a common ideology—which seemed, to
the amazement of many, to be religious in origin, in
character, and in power. This premodern ideological network seemed then, and is now, remarkably
adept at using modern tools to conduct asymmetrical
warfare in which, as the historian Victor Davis Hanson has put it, relatively unsophisticated weapons
like rocket-propelled grenades "permit illiterate
teenagers to kill an American army officer with a
quarter-million-dollar education from West Point,
riding in a $100,000 Humvee."[4] Those same net-
works, it seems clear, would not hesitate to escalate
the violence to a qualitatively new level, by using
weapons of mass destruction, should they acquire
them.[5]

As Walter Laqueur writes, a certain "psychological
resistance against accepting uncomfortable facts" is
a staple of the human condition. That commonplace
defense mechanism has surely been in play in America since 9/11. But the difficulties it causes have been
compounded, in and out of government, by other
misconceptions. There is the "wretched of the earth"
detour from reality, which misapprehends what hit
us on 9/11 as the product of economic deprivation
and urges us to address the "root causes" of terrorism. There is an understandable reluctance, among

many, to accept the possibility that what Samuel Huntington famously described as a "clash of civilizations" may be upon us—as there is a fear that an imprudent politician might trigger just such a clash, were he or she to describe our circumstances in those terms.[6] Of even more importance in befogging our understanding, however, has been the tendency—again, both in and out of government—to assume a form of secularization theory and persuade ourselves that whatever is happening to reshape the twenty-first century *can't* be happening in the religious terms, and for the religious reasons, described by its perpetrators: that's just too, well, primitive. *It can't be happening this way*, we tell ourselves. There *must* be some other explanation.

Now, however, more than a half decade after 9/11, there are certain things we cannot *not* understand. For unless we grasp the character of this new kind of war, its religious and ideological roots, the passions that have grown from those roots, and our current vulnerabilities to those passions, our chances of prevailing against an adversary with a radically different view of the human future—and a willingness, even eagerness, to die for the sake of hastening that future—are weakened. In several senses, then, the perpetrators of 9/11 did us an unintentional favor: 9/11 compelled the United States to address the way in which the new enemy, essentially parasitic on the modern state, had quietly begun to conquer countries that it turned into hosts from which to launch its attacks—like Afghanistan and parts of Pakistan. Even more important, in terms of clarifying what we must face over the long haul, 9/11 forced us to see what we had hitherto refused to see: that we are now confronted by an existential enemy, that is, one for whom a greater share in the world's wealth or power may be a subsidiary goal, but whose primary motivation is the overthrow of our very way of life—our civilization.[7]

The war in which we now find ourselves began before 9/11. We did not recognize its opening shots for what they were when fatwas authorizing the murder of all Americans were issued from caves in the Hindu Kush, or when American embassies were bombed in East Africa, or when, in the port of Aden, the USS *Cole* had a huge hole blown in its side by al-Qaeda operatives who had rigged themselves into human torpedoes. The war is now being fought on multiple fronts, with more likely to come. Many are interconnected: there is an Afghan front, an Iraqi front, an Iranian front, a Lebanese/Syrian front, a Gaza front, a Somali front, a Pakistani front, a North Africa/Maghreb front, a Sudanese front, a Southeast Asian front, an intelligence front, a financial-flows front, an economic front, an energy front, and a homeland security front. These are all fields of fire—some kinetic, others of a different sort—in the same global war, and they must be understood as such. Al-Qaeda attacks on the United States and on American diplomatic and military assets were, for example, planned in the Philippines and other parts of Southeast Asia. Places unknown to the vast majority of Americans are now among the most evil places on earth, as one U.S. Special Forces officer puts it; what happens in locales previously unknown save in the most recondite geography bees–North Waziristan– has direct effects on our armed forces in Afghanistan, Iraq, and elsewhere. What is being plotted in such places could have devastating effects on the homeland.[8]

Bernard Lewis, the English-speaking world's preeminent scholar of the history of Islam, was reflecting on all this and noted the difference between our times and the days when he worked for British intelligence, during the darkest period of World War II. Then, he told the *Wall Street Journal,* "we knew who we were, we knew who the enemy was, we knew the dangers and the issues. It is different today. We don't know who we are. We don't know the issues, and we still do not understand the nature of the enemy."[9] Not knowing, and worse, not *wanting* to know, is lethal. That was proven beyond any doubt on 9/11; any similar events in the future will provide an exclamation point to what we should have grasped by now.

Now, as we approach the end of the first decade of the twenty-first century, there are more things we cannot *not* know. My purpose here is to identify what we should have learned, since September 11,

2001: about the enemy, about us—and about what must be done to see us through to a future safe for freedom.

These fifteen lessons can be clustered under three headings: Understanding the Enemy, Rethinking Realism, and Deserving Victory.

PART ONE

UNDERSTANDING

THE

ENEMY

LESSON 1. The great human questions, including the great questions of public life, are ultimately theological.

How men and women think about God–or don't think about God–has a great deal to do with how they envision the just society, and how they determine the appropriate means by which to build that society. This means taking theology seriously–which includes taking seriously others' concepts of God's nature and purposes, and their commitments to the beliefs arising from those concepts–as well as the theologies that have shaped the civilization of the West. If we have not learned *this* over the past five years, one wonders if we have learned anything.

Yet that very question–what have we learned?–arises every time a commentator or politician or statesman uses "theology" as a synonym for "superstition," or "theological" as a contempt-riddled substitute for "mindless." Such glib (and truly mindless) usages must stop; they are an impediment to clear thinking about our situation. And our situation is too urgent for muddleheadedness arising from prejudice.

Failures on this front tend toward the comprehensive, not least because American education has done a very poor job of equipping Americans with a minimal comprehension of the teachings of the world's great religions. The problem is particularly urgent, however, in those parts of the United States Government where a genteel secularity is the analytic default position—and the received wisdom on How To Understand Things As They Are. This puts American diplomacy and intelligence collection at an immense disadvantage in a world in which the true curiosities—the things that really need explaining—are not throngs of Mexican pilgrims at the shrine of Our Lady of Guadalupe, or several million Hindus ritually bathing in the Ganges, or the *Hajj* to Mecca, or the Shiite pilgrimage to Karbala. The curiosities, the things that need explaining as cutting strangely against the human grain, are those redoubts of aggressive and inward-looking secularism to be found in, for example, western higher education and journalism.

Tone deafness to the fact that for the overwhelming majority of humanity, religious conviction provides *the* story line through which life's meaning is read is, in one sense, a by-product of a disinclination to acknowledge the truth of what has become something of a cliché: that "ideas have consequences." They do, manifestly, and understanding the consequential ideas that shape a given historical epoch, and their interplay, is essential to wise statecraft. We understood this during the Cold War, which was, at bottom, a global contest of fundamental ideas: ideas about human nature, ideas about human community, ideas about human origins, human aspirations, human destiny. Understanding that the contest with communism was idea-driven, the West, led by the United States, deployed intellectual and cultural resources as well as military power to blunt the threat that communism posed, to expose it for what it was, and, ultimately, to defeat it. There would seem to be a lesson here.

The idea of inevitable progress in history–the idea that the human story is inevitably unfolding in such a way that the future will always be better than the present and the past–has exercised such a profound grip on the modern American imagination that we may have forgotten that it is, at best, a hypothesis, not a given of the human condition. Things can, and do, get worse, especially when cultural morale declines: much of Europe today exhibits a kind of cultural exhaustion that does not bode well for the future. Moreover, as Aldous Huxley presciently saw in *Brave New World*, technology can lead to real reverses in human affairs–indeed, to the deterioration of our very idea of humanity. All of which is to suggest that the holiday from history, and from the obligation to press history in a more human direction, that Americans seemed to take in the aftermath of the Cold War is a snare and a delusion. History must be *made* to march in the direction of genuine human progress; world affairs have no intrinsic momentum that necessarily results in the victory of decency. Maintaining the morale necessary to achieving progress in history requires us to live our lives, today, against a moral horizon of responsibility that is wider and deeper than the quest for personal satisfactions. The future of our civilization does not rest merely on the advance of material wealth and technological prowess; the future of the West turns on the question of whether our spiritual aspirations are noble or base.

It is, perhaps, ironic that, at precisely the moment when a religiously grounded, existential threat to the civilization of the West has manifested itself with real power, a new atheism, dripping with disdain for traditional religious conviction, has risen up in the form of broadsides by bestselling polemicists like Richard Dawkins, Daniel Dennett, Christopher Hitchens, and Sam Harris.[1] Yet contrary to the claims of these new atheists and their call to the "maturity" of unbelief, a West that has lost the ability to think in terms of "God" and "Satan," and that has forgotten the drama contained in the idea of "redemption," is a West that will be at a loss to recognize what inspires and empowers those enemies of the West who showed their bloody hand on September 11, 2001. A West that does not take religious ideas seriously as a dynamic force in the world's unfolding history is a West that will have disarmed itself, conceptually and imaginatively, in the midst of war.

LESSON 2. To speak of Judaism, Christianity, and Islam as the "three Abrahamic faiths," the "three religions of the Book," or the "three monotheisms" obscures rather than illuminates. These familiar tropes ought to be retired.

There are, of course, some obvious truths here. Viewed from the perspective of Buddhism, Hinduism, or Shinto, the faiths of Judaism, Christianity, and Islam, while clearly "other," exhibit many "familial" characteristics that may seem to make them cousins of sorts. Moreover, and more important in terms of their own self-understanding, Judaism, Christianity, and Islam all trace their origins to the self-revelation of the one, true God to Abraham. What has emerged from that common point of origin is, however, decisively different—especially with regard to Islam.

In recent years, it has been frequently suggested that there is a relationship between Christianity and Islam that is analogous—some would say, virtually identical—to what Rabbi David Novak has called the "common border" between Judaism and Christianity.[1] Islamic regard for Abraham and Moses, Jesus and Mary is often cited as an example of this alleged affinity. Yet as the eminent French scholar Alain Besançon has pointed out,

> The Abraham of Genesis is not the Ibrahim of the Qur'an; Moses is not Moussa. As for Jesus, he appears, as Issa, out of place and out of time, without reference to the landscape of Israel. His mother, Mary, or Mariam, identified as the sister of Aaron, gives birth to him under a palm tree. Then Issa performs several miracles, which seem to have been drawn from the apocryphal gospels, and announces the future coming of Muhammad.
>
> Jesus is indeed granted a position of honor in the Qur'an, but this Jesus is not the Jesus in whom Christians proclaim their faith. The Jesus/Issa of the Qur'an promulgates the same message as the earlier prophets—Adam, Abraham, Lot, and the rest. Indeed, all possess the same knowledge and proclaim the same message, which is Islam. Like the rest, Issa is sent to preach the oneness of God. He is emphatically no Trinitarian, not an "associator"; "do not say Three," he protests. Nor is he the son of God, but a simple mortal. Nor is he a mediator between earthly men and their heavenly Father, because Islam knows not the concept of

mediation. Nor, since in Islam it is unimagin-
able that a messenger of God can be van-
quished, does he die on the cross; a double is
substituted for him.[2]

Besançon's reference to what appear to be
Qur'anic borrowings from the apocryphal gospels
raises, for a twenty-first-century audience, the question posed by St. John Damascene in the eighth century: that is, whether Islam ought to be understood,
in terms of the history of religions, as a heretical off-
shoot of Christianity that came into being when defective Christologies (i.e., theologies of the nature,
person, and mission of Christ) intersected with ideas
culled from pre-Islamic Arabic tribal religions and
off-brand forms of Judaism, all of which were then
forged into a new religious system by the genius of
Muhammad.[3] But that is an argument for another
time and place. So is wrestling with St. Thomas
Aquinas's thirteenth-century refusal to concede a
parallelism between Judaism and Christianity, on
the one hand, and Islam, on the other, which was
based on Thomas's conviction that Muhammad
taught great falsehoods.[4] Suffice it to say that Islam's
deep theological structure includes themes that ren-
der the notion of "three Abrahamic faiths" ultimately
misleading in understanding Islam's faith and practice—particularly if this trope is understood in the
popular imagination as a matter of three equivalent
legs propping up a single monotheistic stool.

Take, for example, the question of Islamic supersessionism: Islam's claim that it supersedes Judaism and Christianity, both of which are finally unveiled, in the revelation to Muhammad, as false (or, at best, deeply distorted) religions.[5] This, of course, Christianity cannot accept, for it is a cardinal tenet of Christian doctrine that God's self-revelation culminates in the person and teaching of Jesus Christ; no further revelation can be imagined. This bedrock Christian conviction—that God's revelation has been completed in Christ, in the sense that nothing essential for the world's salvation will be revealed after Christ—also helps identify another defect of the "three Abrahamic faiths" trope. In a Christian understanding of salvation history, Abraham is not only the great ancestor; he also points toward the fulfillment of God's saving purposes, which will emerge from Abraham's stock, the People of Israel—a fulfillment Christians believe God accomplished in Jesus of Nazareth, Son of Abraham and Son of David. From a Christian point of view, Abraham cannot point beyond the fulfillment of the divine promise to Abraham: which is to say, Abraham cannot point toward a post-Christian revelation to Muhammad (or anyone else, for that matter). For Christians, in other words, the word "Abrahamic" does not designate merely origin and patrimony; it includes finality and destiny—Abraham points to what God intended for humanity by choosing Abraham, and that is the gift of God's Son through the People of Israel. (To think

"Abrahamic" solely in terms of origin also poses problems for Jewish self-understanding, but exploring that would take us too far afield here.)

Despite the supersessionist claims that some Christians have made throughout history vis-à-vis Judaism, no orthodox Christian holds that God's self-revelation in Christ negates God's self-revelation in the history of the People of Israel. Islam, by contrast, takes a radically supersessionist view of both Judaism and Christianity, claiming that the final revelation to Muhammad de facto trumps, by way of supersession, any prior revelatory value (so to speak) that might be found in the Hebrew Bible or the Christian New Testament.[6]

Thus Islamic supersessionism has a built-in tendency to set in motion a dynamic of conflict with Judaism and Christianity that is not "required" vis-à-vis Islam by the deep theological structure of Judaism and Christianity—although, to be sure, Christians have taken an aggressive and bloody-minded posture toward Islam on many occasions over the past fourteen hundred years, an aggressiveness that has left deep resentments in the Islamic world and a historic burden of conscience among more thoughtful Christians. Nor should it be thought that Islamic supersessionism *necessarily* requires violent conflict between Islam and "the rest," although that is a face of itself that Islam has displayed throughout its history; and in the contemporary world, that face has led to what Samuel Huntington

describes as Islam's "bloody borders."[7] Still, as Bernard
Lewis writes, "Since its first emergence from Arabia
in the seventh century, Islam has been in almost continuous conflict with Christendom, through the
original Muslim conquests and the Christian recon-
quests, through jihad and crusade, the Turkish advance, and the European expansion. Though Islam
has fought many wars on many frontiers, it was the
wars against Christendom which were the longest
and most devastating, and which came to loom in
Muslim awareness as the great jihad par excel-
lence."[8] That Islamic supersessionism was an important theological source of this "almost continuous
conflict" need not be doubted, although other factors
were obviously in play.

This supersessionism, and the conflicts it has engendered, lead Lewis and others to suggest that we
need a new reading of world history. It is striking to
look through a standard reference work like the
Times Atlas of World History and find so little on Islam, much less on the world-historical ebb and
flow of Islam-versus-the-rest. Yet, Lewis suggests,
that ebb and flow, underwritten by a certain understanding of Islamic supersessionism, is one of the
primary story lines of the last millennium and a
half. To take but one example: We tend to think of
the rise of European colonialism and imperialism
as the product of intra-European economic, political, demographic, and religious dynamics—the
quest for wealth; the Great Power game; the ques-

tion of what to do with younger sons in an age of primogeniture; the missionary imperative. Lewis suggests that we see European expansion as some Muslims likely saw it: as a great flanking movement in response to Islamic advances into the continent of Europe:

> When Vasco da Gama arrived in Calicut he explained that he had come "in search of Christians and spices." It was a fair summary of the motives that had sent the Portuguese to Asia, as perhaps also, with appropriate adjustments, of the jihad to which the Portuguese voyages were a long-delayed reply. The sentiment of Christian struggle was strong among the Portuguese who sailed to the East. The great voyages of discovery were seen as a religious war, a continuation of the Crusades and of the Reconquest, and against the same enemy. In eastern waters, it was Muslim rulers—in Egypt, Turkey, Iran, and India—who were the chief opponents of the Portuguese, and whose domination they ended. After the Portuguese came the other maritime peoples of the West, who together established a west European ascendancy in Africa and southern Asia that lasted until the twentieth century.[9]

Or, as Lewis asks later in his narrative, were the Barbary pirates who so exercised Thomas Jefferson independent operators out for loot, as is suggested by the term "pirates"–and most of our history books? Or are they more accurately understood, in a long view of history, as "privateers" in the ongoing jihad against Christendom, engaging in a maritime form of asymmetrical warfare against the first frigates of the U.S. Navy and the U.S. Marine Corps at a time when Muslim power was in retreat?[10]

Islamic supersessionism is one of the theological ideas that distinguishes Islam from Judaism and Christianity in an important way. It is also an idea that has had profound consequences in history. When an Ottoman Muslim historian referred to the Poles who had come to the rescue of Vienna in 1683 as "the people of hell," he was drawing on one powerful strand of a tradition of religious thought that dated back a millennium–even as he foreshadowed Osama bin Laden.[11]

Islam is further distinguished by its understanding of the nature of its sacred text, the Qur'an, an understanding that further illustrates the deficiencies of the "three monotheistic religions" trope. The English-speaking world owes a great deal, culturally, to the Authorized or King James version of the Bible, whose imprint can be found as far from King James's committee as the Lincoln Memorial in Washington. Yet that debt is minimal compared to the debt that Islam, and Islamic culture, owe to the Qur'an. As one Muslim translator puts it,

The Qur'an was the starting point for all the Islamic sciences: Arabic grammar was developed to serve the Qur'an, the study of Arabic phonetics was pursued in order to determine the exact pronunciation of Qur'anic words, the science of Arabic rhetoric was developed in order to describe the features of the inimitable style of the Qur'an, the art of Arabic calligraphy was cultivated through writing down the Qur'an, the Qur'an is the basis of Islamic law and theology; indeed, as the celebrated fifteenth-century scholar and author Suyuti said, "Everything is based on the Qur'an." The entire religious life of the Muslim world is built around the text of the Qur'an.[12]

The Qur'an is, then, one of the most influential books in the history of humanity. Yet it is Islam's understanding of the Qur'an's origins that further sets Islam in contrast to Judaism and Christianity. For the origin of the Qur'an, as Muslims understand it, is not analogous to the origin of the Bible, according to Judaism and Christianity. That distinction about origins leads to a different understanding of the nature of the sacred text, and thence to further differences.

One prominent Christian understanding of biblical inspiration was expressed by the bishops of the Catholic Church gathered in the Second Vatican

Council in these terms: "The divinely revealed realities, which are contained and presented in the text of sacred Scripture, have been written down under the inspiration of the Holy Spirit. To compose the sacred books, God chose certain men who, all the while he employed them in this task, made full use of their own powers and faculties so that, though he acted in them and by them, it was as true authors that they consigned to writing whatever he wanted written, and no more."[13] That Christian theological understanding of "inspiration"—which would not be foreign to Judaism—provides for the possibility of the interpretation of sacred texts, and indeed for the development of doctrine in light of an evolving understanding of the full meaning of Scripture. The Qur'an, by contrast, is understood by Muslims to be dictated, word for word and syllable for syllable, so that there is no question of "exegesis," as Jews and Christians would use the term; nor is there any possibility of a postscriptural development of doctrine.[14] The priority in Islam is on jurisprudence, the debate of experts in Islamic law on the applicability of texts to circumstances (for example, in the issuing of a fatwa).

The Bible is a moral teacher that calls faithful Jews and Christians to use their reason in understanding the meaning and import of its moral teaching, including the commandments; Abraham, Jacob, Moses, David, many of the prophets, and Jesus himself wrestle with the meaning of God's purposes and commands in the Old and New Testaments. Islam's holy book, by contrast, is described by an influential Egyptian Islamic activist in these terms: "The Qur'an for mankind is like a manual for a machine."[15] Reverence for the Qur'an has produced some of the most beautiful calligraphy the world has ever seen. The Islamic understanding of the Qur'an as dictated does not, however, lend itself easily to other kinds of beauty: the beauty of spiritual and moral wrestling with the meaning of sacred text, and the beauty of insight that comes from that wrestling.[16]

Alain Besançon takes us even further into the heart of the matter when he draws yet another important theological distinction between Judaism and Christianity, on the one hand, and Islam, on the other:

> Although Muslims like to enumerate the 99 names of God, missing from the list, but central to the Jewish and even more so to the Christian concept of God, is "Father"–i.e., a personal God capable of a reciprocal and loving relationship with men. The one God of the Qur'an, the God Who demands submission, is a distant God; to call him "Father" would be an anthropomorphic sacrilege. The Muslim God is utterly impassive; to ascribe loving feeling to Him would be suspect.[17]

If God is not "Father," then it is difficult to imagine
the human person as having been made "in the image of God." And that, in turn, puts great strain on any
idea of an intimacy between faith and reason. In Judaism and Christianity, men and women are bound
to God in many ways, including speech and argument. To take the primal example: in Genesis, God
"speaks" forth his creation; Adam's speech, by which
he names the animals, gives the primordial man his
first hint of his distinctive status in creation and of his
distinctive relationship to the creator. In Islam, by
contrast, participation in the Creator's creative work
is not a characteristic of the human-divine relationship, which is defined by submission to the majesty
of God, who neither begets nor is begotten (as the in-
scriptions inside the magnificent Dome of the Rock
in Jerusalem remind the visitor or pilgrim). According to Islam, the Jewish and Christian understanding
of God limits God's omnipotence.[18]

Thus, from a theological point of view, Islam is
"other" in relationship to Christianity and Judaism
in a way that Christianity and Judaism cannot be to
one another. These theological differences help explain the dramatically different stance that Judaism,
Christianity, and Islam take toward conversions
from their communities. Jews mourn the conversion
of a Jew to Christianity, as Christians mourn the
conversion of one of their number to Judaism. But
this is mourning within the family, as it were: the
Jewish convert to Christianity is understood to have

prematurely identified the Messiah for whose coming both Jews and Christians long; the Christian
convert to Judaism is thought to have misunderstood
the fulfillment of the Law and the Prophets in Jesus
Christ. The Muslim convert to Judaism or Christianity is, by contrast, liable at least in principle to death.

The late Pope John Paul II, whom much of the
world recognized as an apostle of genuine interreligious dialogue, recognized this difference. In one of
his most personal statements, the international bestseller *Crossing the Threshold of Hope*, John Paul (so
often contrasted since April 2005 with his "hard-
line" successor) expressed his admiration for "the
religiosity of Muslims" and his admiration for their
"fidelity to prayer." As he put it, "The image of believers in Allah who, without caring about time or place,
fall to their knees and immerse themselves in prayer
remains a model for all those who invoke the true
God, in particular for those Christians who, having
deserted their magnificent cathedrals, pray only a
little or not at all." But prior to this, John Paul II had
cut to the core theological issue:

> Whoever knows the Old and New Testaments,
> and then reads the Qur'an, clearly sees the
> process by which it completely reduces Divine
> Revelation. It is impossible not to note the
> movement away from what God said about
> himself, first in the Old Testament through the
> Prophets, and then finally in the New Testa-

ment through His Son. In Islam, all the richness of God's self-revelation, which constitutes the heritage of the Old and New Testaments, has definitely been set aside.

Some of the most beautiful names in the human language are given to the God of the Qur'an, but He is ultimately a God outside of the world, a God who is only Majesty, never Emmanuel, God with us. Islam is not a religion of redemption. There is no room for the Cross and the Resurrection. Jesus is mentioned, but only as a prophet who prepares for the last prophet, Muhammad. There is also mention of Mary, His Virgin Mother, but the tragedy of redemption is completely absent. For this reason not only the theology but also the anthropology of Islam is very distant from Christianity.[19]

Islamic theological anthropology—Islam's theologically driven concept of the human person—yields, in turn, a view of the just society that seems to be different from that of Judaism and Christianity. Islamic theological anthropology is one root of what Efraim Karsh has termed "the fusion of religious and temporal authority" in Islam, a fusion that is not peripheral to Islamic self-understanding. That fusion has, in turn, led to what Karsh calls "Islam's millenarian imperial experience"—and, one might add, the millenarian political expectations of some Muslims today. Islamic theological anthropology also helps explain Islam's traditional division of the human world into the "House of Islam," the "God-hallowed realm" that embodies God's purposes on earth, and the "House of War," which is composed of all those who have not yet submitted to Allah and his Prophet. From there, it is but a short step to the Muslim conviction that, as Bernard Lewis writes, "The Islamic state [is] the only truly legitimate power on earth and the Islamic community the sole repository of truth and enlightenment, surrounded on all sides by an outer darkness of barbarism and unbelief."[20]

That theological anthropology, and the fusion of religious and temporal authority to which it leads, is also one of the roots of Islam's difficulties in creating the cultural conditions for the possibility of social pluralism, which sociologist Peter Berger defines as "the coexistence in civic peace of different racial, ethnic, and religious groups, with social interaction between them."[21] Indeed, it is difficult to imagine genuine pluralism—"creeds intelligibly in conflict," as John Courtney Murray describes it, or the engagement of differences within the bond of civility, to cite Richard John Neuhaus's formula—in a classic Islamic conception of the just society. For in the just society as classic Islam envisions it, even the "peoples of the Book," those Jews and Christians who are putatively the other two legs on the monotheistic stool, are second-class citizens: *dhimmis*, whose social, economic, and political circumstances eventu-

ally deteriorate to the point where conversion becomes a means of survival.[22]

Islam's concept of the just society was also deeply
influenced by its foundational historical experience.
As Bernard Lewis puts it, "The Founder of Islam
was his own Constantine, and founded his own state
and empire. He did not therefore create–or need to
create–a church. The dichotomy of *regnum* and *sacerdotium*, so crucial in the history of Western
Christendom, had no equivalent in Islam."[23] In the
English-speaking world, we often think of Magna
Carta–the enforcement of limitations on autocratic
royal power by the nobility of England–as the starting point for what would evolve into western liberties. Yet a strong case can be made that the more
decisive moment took place in 1076, 139 years before
King John conceded to the English barons. For when
Pope Gregory VII excommunicated the emperor
Henry IV and set in motion a process that confirmed
the independence of the Catholic Church from the
power of the state in the ordering of the Church's internal affairs, he set firmly in the cultural subsoil of
the West a distinction between political and priestly
power. Why was that "dichotomy" of *regnum* and
sacerdotium, political power and spiritual authority,
so crucial in the history of the West? Because, by putting limits on political power, it created conditions
for the possibility of the social pluralism of the medieval world, which in turn shaped the public terrain
from which democracy eventually grew.[24]

It goes—or should go—without saying that Islam has, over the centuries, given meaning and purpose to hundreds of millions of lives that have been nobly and decently lived. Islam has given the world architectural and decorative beauty, magnificent poetry, a lived experience of racial comity that puts a lot of the rest of the world to shame, important philosophers, a profound mystical tradition, and much, much more. Yet it is also true that, throughout the world today, Islam is in the midst of what Alain Besançon aptly describes as "a long-delayed, wrenching, and still far from accomplished encounter with modernity."[25] That struggle with modernity created, as we shall see in a moment, a struggle within Islam, an intra-Islamic civil war. When that struggle spilled out from the House of Islam, it became one of the defining dynamics of the history of our time—and eventually left a great gash in the ground in lower Manhattan.

The Islamic encounter with modernity has been so wrenching—and so volatile—because it intensified, even as it reflected, certain problems built deep into the theological structure of Islam from the beginning. That, in turn, led to patterns of confrontation that seem, at the moment, qualitatively different from the strained relationship between Christianity and modernity in the early phase of their encounter. In fact, and despite the conflicts of the Enlightenment and the Age of Revolution in Europe, Christianity's convictions about the rationality built into the world by the world's creator were one important source of "modernity," if by that term we mean the scientific method, historical-critical study of ancient texts, and government by the arts of persuasion, to take but three examples. Are there, in Islam's theological self-understanding, themes analogous to Christianity's theologically driven convictions about the rationality of the world, themes that could, over time, make Islam's encounter with modernity fruitful for both Islam and for the modern world? The answer to that question will play a large role in shaping the course of the human future. Whether Islam can evolve into a religion capable of providing religious warrants for genuine pluralism is–to take the most immediately urgent issue–one of the great questions on which the future of the twenty-first century will turn.

That question engages both Islam's distinctive history and questions of theological anthropology deeply embedded in the structure of Islamic self-understanding. Those questions further underscore the disutility of the idea of the "three Abrahamic faiths"–a notion invented by twentieth-century intellectuals, not an idea with any deep roots in Islamic (or Christian, or Jewish) thought.[26]

LESSON 3. Jihadism is the enemy in the multifront war that has been declared upon us.

There are many forms of Islam. Some of them, often called "fundamentalism" or "Islamism," stress the need for a deep religious and moral reform within the House of Islam and the reestablishment of Islamic political power. The specific form of Islamism that threatens the West–and with which we are engaged in an unavoidable contest to define the human future–is best described as *jihadism*. Jihadism is distinguished from other forms of Islamism or the ill-named "Islamic fundamentalism" by its distinctive views on Islamic reform, by its political methods and goals (which are messianic and involve nothing less than a global Islamic state), by its concept of its enemies, and by the methods it legitimates for dealing with those enemies.

Jihadism has been defined succinctly and well by Richard John Neuhaus: "Jihadism is the religiously inspired ideology [which teaches] that it is the moral obligation of all Muslims to employ whatever means

[are] necessary to compel the world's submission to Islam."[1]

That, I suggest, is naming the enemy correctly: those who hold this view are, de facto, in a state of belligerency against the rest of the world. Neuhaus goes on to note, "It will be objected that, in the Qur'an, jihad can also mean peaceful spiritual struggle. That is true, as it is true that those Muslims who believe jihad means peaceful spiritual struggle are not the enemy."[2] That the jihadists understand jihad as Neuhaus describes it cannot be doubted, however, because this is precisely what they claim. Indeed, another of those questions on which the history of the twenty-first century and beyond will turn is the question of whether the jihadists' definition becomes the most culturally assertive definition of jihad within the many worlds of Islam. That is a development that both Muslims and non-Muslims must resist.

Once we have recognized that, the next requirement for all concerned is to understand the theological roots of those claims.

LESSON 4. Jihadism has a complex intellectual history, the chief points of which must be grasped in order to understand the nature of the threat it poses to the West.

While jihadism is an expression of Islam's struggle with modernity, its deeper roots reach back to an Islamic sense of failure that antedates the onset of modernity. Islam's original conquests, and the second wave of Islamic insurgency that culminated at the Battle of Vienna in 1683, were both halted by the forces of Christendom. Those reverses led to a nineteenth- and twentieth-century colonial experience in which most of the world's Muslims were ruled by people Muslims regarded as inferiors and infidels—an experience of humiliation exacerbated by the tensions engendered by the Islamic encounter with modernity. The world had not turned out the way it should have. Spiritual dissonance, followed by cognitive dissonance, followed.

One can see traces of that sense of failure—and the frustrations caused by the seeming inability to do anything about it—in the inertia that was often said to be the principal characteristic of the Ottoman Empire before its dissolution in the wake of World War I. In fact, though, that inertia had a far longer pedigree. The details are beyond our scope here, but the crucial move was a kind of suspension of intellectual inquiry, which seems to have led to a loss of intellectual vitality, in a Muslim world that had once fostered a lively intellectual life; that had found room within itself for an incorporation of the wisdom of the classical and Persian worlds; and that had created a civilization that was, in many respects, far more advanced than anything Christendom could offer in the early Middle Ages.[1]

In the beginning of the second millennium, intellectual creativity and real argument were possible in the Islamic world. As Frederick Copleston, the historian of philosophy, puts it, "The Arabian philosophy was one of the principal channels whereby the complete Aristotle was introduced to the West; but the great philosophers of medieval Islam, men like Avicenna and Averroes, were more than mere transmitters or even commentators; they changed and developed the philosophy of Aristotle, more or less according to the spirit of neo-Platonism."[2] Then something happened, and during the middle centuries of the second millennium the spirit of inquiry seemed to dry up in the House of Islam.

It is interesting to speculate on the possibility that this general pattern may have had a specific point of origin in the work of the great Averroes (Ibn Rushd), whom medieval Christian scholars referred to with intellectual reverence as "The Commentator." Convinced that Aristotle was the final repository of human wisdom, Averroes, who died in exile in Morocco in 1198, "[made] theology subordinate to philosophy . . . [and] the latter the judge of the former, so that it belongs to the philosopher to decide what theological doctrines need to be allegorically interpreted and in what way they should be interpreted."[3] But wherever we locate the origin of the inertia, Islamic religious authorities eventually became nervous about such philosophical speculations; and that nervousness, combined with Islam's traditional sense of self-sufficiency (as well as its disdain for the achievements of the infidel world), created a cultural situation that eventually led to a deterioration of intellectual vitality. As Bernard Lewis writes, "the Renaissance, the Reformation, the scientific revolution, and the Enlightenment . . . passed without effect in the Islamic world, without even being noticed." Over time, that pattern of intellectual stagnation in Islam would yield drastic results.[4] Thus in 2002, a study of "Arab Human Development," organized by Arab intellectuals and published under the auspices of the United Nations, found that "the Arab world translates about 330 books annually, one-fifth of the number that Greece translates. The accumulative total of translated books [into Arabic] since [the ninth century] is about 100,000." More books are translated into Spanish in an average decade or two than have been translated into Arabic in a millennium.[5]

The causal chain that takes us from medieval Islamic debates about philosophy, law, and the boundaries of speculative religious thought to the caves of Tora Bora and 9/11 involves numerous figures, among whom perhaps the most important are the scholars Ahmad ibn 'Abd al-Halim ibn Taymiyya (1263–1328) and Muhammad ibn 'Abd al-Wahhab (1703/4–1792), and two contemporary activist-theorists, Hasan al-Banna (1906–1949) and Sayyid Qutb (1903–1966).

We can begin to make a long story manageably short with some evocative scene setting by Bernard Lewis:

> In the middle of the thirteenth century, a new move westward was planned and executed by the Mongols. Prince Hülegü, a grandson of Jenghiz Khan, crossed the Oxus with orders from the great khan to conquer all the lands of Islam as far as Egypt. Within a few months, the long-haired Mongol horsemen thundered across Persia, overcoming all resistance, and in January 1258 converged on the city of Baghdad. They stormed, looted, and burned the old caliphal capital, and on the 20th February 1258 the last caliph, with as many members of his family as could be found, was put to death. For the first time since the

days of the Prophet, a non-Muslim people had invaded the heartlands of Islam, destroyed the great historic institution of the caliphate and established a pagan domination over the believers.[6]

Desperate circumstances seemed to call for desperate measures, based on a particularly stringent interpretation of Islam. Thus, as the Mongols were raping, pillaging, murdering, and burning their way across the Islamic world, Ahmad ibn 'Abd al-Halim ibn Taymiyya taught that the survival of Islam required political power; that the pursuit of that power could, indeed should, be undertaken by the use of armed force (a corruption, I should note, of the just war tradition); and that jihad involved both an absolute love of God and a parallel "absolute hatred" for all that God proscribes. Mary Habeck also notes that ibn Taymiyya broadened the targets of jihad to include "not only heretics, apostates, hypocrites, sinners, and unbelievers (including Christians and Jews) . . . but also any Muslim who tried to avoid participating in jihad"[7]–thus adumbrating the intra-Islamic civil war that has now spilled over into jihadism's struggle against the rest of the world. The result was what Walter Laqueur has dubbed the "Taymiyya approach" to Islam-and-the-rest, which is "based on the assumption that peace and a just social order will only prevail in the world once Islam has been victorious worldwide, for all other religions and ideologies want to persecute the true believers and aim at the defeat and downfall of Islam."[8]

Muhammad ibn 'Abd al-Wahhab is slightly more familiar to alert westerners because his form of Islam became the official Islam of the Kingdom of Saudi Arabia, from which it has been exported around the world on the wings of Saudi gold—the "rest of the world" including madrassas in the Detroit metropolitan area and the chaplain services of American prisons. Wahhab emphasized the radical unicity (oneness) and lordship of God, whose relationship to the world is that of an absolute lawgiver: God relates to the world through his will, and there is no spiritual wrestling, so to speak, with the divine will—there is only submission. True submission, according to Wahhab, requires both a profound disdain for Islamic mysticism and the destruction of any human artifacts that are thought to embody or express divine attributes (thus the Wahhabi-influenced Taliban's destruction of the Bamyan Buddhas in Afghanistan). Yet Wahhab had little influence in his own time, or indeed for centuries afterward. It would take a vast transfer of western wealth to Saudi Arabia to make Wahhabism a potent force in shaping the human future.[9]

Hasan al-Banna, Egyptian founder of the Muslim Brotherhood, set himself against those Islamic modernizers of the early twentieth century who, as Mary Habeck notes, came in a variety of forms: socialists, liberals, and nationalists. Al-Banna condemned the

"mental colonization" of Islam under colonial rule
and urged a struggle against a West that he perceived as having thus far won a "ruthless war whose
battlefield has been the spirits and souls of Muslims
as well as their beliefs and intellects, exactly as it has
triumphed on the political and military battlefields."[10]
Since this could only have happened because of the
corruptions of Muslim life, al-Banna proposed an Islamic social reformation. The educational, social,
economic, religious, and charitable activities of the
Muslim Brotherhood would be one form of this reformation. Jihad would be another, for God had given
Muslims the privilege and duty of saving the world
from its errors. After cleansing the House of Islam,
true Muslims would cleanse their territories of infidels and unbelievers, beginning with al-Banna's
own Egypt, and then move on. Where? Hasan al-
Banna, who believed that Islam was "both a religion
and a state," such that the Qur'an and the sword
were "inseparable," was a man of no small dreams:

> Our task . . . is to stand against the flood of
> modernist civilization overflowing from the
> swamp of materialistic and sinful desires. This
> flood has swept the Muslim nation away from
> the Prophet's leadership and Qur'anic guid-
> ance and deprived the world of its guiding
> light. Western secularism moved into a Mus-
> lim world already estranged from its Qur'anic
> roots, and delayed its advancement for cen-

turies, and will continue to do so until we drive
it from our lands. Moreover, we will not stop at
this point, but will pursue this evil force to its
own lands, invade its Western heartland, and
struggle to overcome it until all the world
shouts by the name of the Prophet and the
teachings of Islam spread throughout the
world. Only then will Muslims achieve their
fundamental goal, and there will be no more
"persecution" and all religion will be exclusively for Allah.[11]

Sayyid Qutb, through whom these currents of
thought were brought to a finely honed point of development with world-historical consequences, was
a forty-five-year-old exchange scholar, an Egyptian
literary critic and educational theorist, when he sailed
to the United States in the first-class stateroom of one
of the great Atlantic liners in 1948. Lawrence Wright
describes him in these terms:

He was western in so many ways—his dress,
his love of classical music and Hollywood
movies. He had read, in translation, the works
of Darwin and Einstein, Byron and Shelley,
and had immersed himself in French literature, especially Victor Hugo. Even before his
journey, however, he worried about the advance of an all-engulfing western civilization.
Despite his erudition, he saw the West as a sin-

gle cultural entity. The distinctions between capitalism and Marxism, Christianity and Judaism, fascism and democracy were insignificant by comparison with the single great divide in Qutb's mind: Islam and the East on the one side, and the Christian West on the other.[12]

Qutb's experiences in the United States sharpened, rather than blunted, his sense of Islam-versus-the-West (and Islam-versus-the-rest). He was appalled at being propositioned by a tipsy fellow passenger (female) on his transatlantic voyage. He was further scandalized when he attended the Colorado State College of Education in Greeley; there, in 1949, he attended a church social, which seems to have been something of turning point in his life and his perceptions of the West. Greeley, Colorado, was a dry town in 1949; full of churches, it seems an unlikely den of iniquity in those days. Yet Qutb was deeply disturbed by the scene in a church hall: "The room convulsed with the feverish music from the gramophone ["Baby, It's Cold Outside," a tune from an Esther Williams movie]. Dancing naked legs filled the hall. Arms draped around the waists, chests met chests, lips met lips, and the atmosphere was full of love . . . the minister paused to watch his young charges swaying to the rhythms of this seductive song." As Lawrence Wright notes, this was "the man–decent, proud, tormented, self-righteous–whose lonely genius would unsettle Islam, threaten regimes across the Muslim world, and beckon to a generation of rootless young Arabs who were looking for meaning and purpose in their lives and would find it in jihad."[13]

Qutb brought together the various lines of jihadist thought noted above in a singularly influential way. He, too, stressed the centrality of God's will in God's relationship to the world, God as the unique and sole lawmaker; for Qutb, liberal political thought (even conservative liberal political thought of a Burkean sort) was a false religion, not simply bad politics. The index of whether a state was truly Muslim was thus the degree to which shari'a law prevailed. Like others before him, but in a harsher way, Qutb stressed that those Muslims who did not live authentic Islamic lives (as he understood the term) were enemies to be fought and, if necessary, killed, as were Jews, Christians, and unbelievers, whose existence was a permanent and necessarily aggressive threat to the success of Islam, exactly as it had been from the beginning. For Sayyid Qutb, "the struggle was not about territory but about truth and which truth would prevail in the world."[14]

In the world-historical view of Sayyid Qutb, nothing really changed. His was a mind literally frozen in time, a mind in which the Crusades and the Spanish *Reconquista* were ongoing, ever-present realities, summoning forth a perpetual struggle, violent if necessary, until the final, global triumph of Islam. Qutb was surely no believer in the idea of "three Abrahamic faiths"; for him, other religions were not simply mistaken, they were evil, "filth" to be expunged.[15] And while his teaching was not that of a scholar deeply versed in Islamic philosophy and law, but that of an autodidact activist, it would resonate with many. After he died what his followers could only regard as a martyr's death in 1964–he was hanged by the Nasser government of Egypt–his mantle was assumed by the likes of the blind sheikh Omar Abdul Rahman, who taught that the source of the world's evil and the greatest of threats to Islam was the United States, which should be struck again and again by jihadists who would not fear to be labeled "terrorists."[16]

There have been many attempts to explain jihadism psychologically; reading the story of Sayyid Qutb, one does experience temptations to psychoanalyze. Succumbing to that temptation would be a mistake, however. For, irrespective of the particularities of individual cases, the power of jihadism–and the distinctive character of the threat it poses–derives from its theological roots. As Pope Benedict XVI pointed out in a lecture at the University of Regensburg in September 2006, the key theological move that underwrites today's jihadist ideology (and practice) is the identification by jihadists of God as Absolute Will. If that is what jihadists believe God to be (irrespective of the degree of warrant that concept can find in classical Islam, which is disputed), then jihadists are, within their own frame of reference, justified in believing that God can command anything—even the irrational. And so, in an extension of the thought of Sayyid Qutb, contemporary jihadists believe that the murder of innocents is not simply morally acceptable, but morally required, if such murders advance the cause of Islam. Thus the origins of one of today's most lethal weapons, the so-called suicide bomber (who, as Fouad Ajami insists, is more properly called the "homicide bomber"), is in a defective, hypervoluntarist concept of the nature of God. This deeply distorted understanding of the God of Abraham leads jihadists and those influenced by jihadist thinking to other theological distortions.

Mercy, for example, comes to be understood as weakness. Thus, in a 2006 Saudi television interview, the program host asked Abdallah al-Bishi, an official Saudi executioner, if he had ever had a "difficult beheading"—say, of a friend. Al-Bishi replied, "Yes, I have beheaded many people who were my friends, but whoever commits an offense brings it upon himself. . . . If I felt compassion for the person I was executing, he would suffer. If the heart is compassionate, the hand fails." Asked if he needed a break during multiple executions, al-Bishi replied, "Allah be praised, there is nothing to it. Three, four, five, six—there is nothing to it. It's entirely normal." Asked if his son, Badr, was being trained in the family profession, al-Bishi replied, "Allah be praised,

Badr is about to be appointed to the position in Riyadh."[17]

Similarly, the concept of justice, one of the four cardinal virtues in Christian moral theology, is traduced by jihadism's defective concept of God into sheer revenge–a process vividly on display in Iraq today. Given Sayyid Qutb's conviction that Islam, rightly understood, and modernity were "utterly incompatible," and given the defective theology that undergirded Qutb's worldview, what seems incomprehensible to so many westerners–the "death cult" that forms "the core of al-Qaeda" and similar entities–begins, within a jihadist frame of reference, to make a certain perverse sense.[18]

While there are parallels here to aspects of what Australian scholar Michael Casey has called "the totalitarian variant of political religion" in the great twentieth-century tyrannies–in particular, "integralism and intolerance, the sanctification of violence in the service of human regeneration, and the denial of individual autonomy" (in the sense of rational moral choice)–jihadism is something different. Jihadism creates a theologically warranted "world without limits" in which the battlefield "now spans pizzerias, buses, public squares, commuter trains . . . subway stations"–and a Jewish center in one of the epicenters of American multiculturalism, Seattle; a world without limits in which a Turkish film, *Valley of the Wolves*, depicts an American Jew harvesting organs at Abu Ghraib for resale; a world without limits in which Hezbollah rocketeers routinely shelter themselves behind UN "peacekeepers" and Lebanese families; a world without limits in which the Palestinian state press mocks the secretary of state of the United States for her race and appearance; and so forth, and so on, in a seeming infinity of variants on the instruction posted by the Taliban religious police: "Throw reason to the dogs–it stinks of corruption."[19]

The line of Islamic thought from Taymiyya and Wahhab that would later influence Hasan al-Banna and Sayyid Qutb was one in which several struggles were being played out–Islam versus modernity; jihadists versus other Islamic reformers; Islam-versus-the-rest. That line of thought came to one terminus when Ayman al-Zawahiri and Osama bin Laden–an Egyptian and a Saudi, a veteran political operator and propagandist and a somewhat dreamy charismatic leader–joined forces to form al-Qaeda [The Base].

The result was something new, and something terribly dangerous: global jihad.[20]

LESSON 5. Jihadists read history and politics through the prism of their distinctive theological convictions, not through the lens of western assumptions about the progressive dynamic of history.

Jihadists read the 1990s, not as the triumph of democracy and certainly not as "the end of history," but as a decade that revealed fatal western weaknesses. To jihadists, the Soviet defeat in Afghanistan (irrespective of the fact that it was made possible in no small part by western aid and technology) meant that modernity was on the run: as Walter Laqueur writes, "the war in Afghanistan had lasted for about ten years; radical Islamists, flush with enthusiasm, thought that it might take only another decade to overthrow the present Arab and Muslim governments and yet another few years to defeat America and the West." The Soviet defeat in Afghanistan also gave birth to what Laqueur calls "the mystique of Muslim invincibility" and, on the strategic side, a "Muslim Brezhnev Doctrine," according to which "all countries that had been occupied by Muslims at one time or another were to be restored to Allah's fold." But this was a dynamic strategic doctrine, according to which, as it were, what's mine is mine and what's yours will be mine in due course. For, according to the new, post-Afghanistan jihadists, "jihad should continue until Allah alone is worshiped by all mankind." Moreover, the final victory of Islam was near; the messianic age, which even the most fervent dreamers had once consigned to a far-distant future, now seemed within grasp.[1] "The Base" that was al-Qaeda was built on the foundation of this strategic conviction: that "there was no chance to build a society based on truly Islamic principles unless the power of the West was broken." That conviction led, in turn, to the tactic of choice, which was jihad: "The rule of Islam, peace and general well-being, could be established only by means of jihad, holy war." And in that war, it was not only necessary that western political and economic power be defeated; "western ideas and concepts had to be decisively refuted" as well.[2]

These strategic and tactical convictions, which drew on ancient warrants even as they were sharpened by the experience of resistance to Soviet power in Afghanistan, provoked new patterns of aggression in the 1990s, which were reinforced when the generally feckless response of the United States to jihadist attacks on our embassies in Kenya and Tanzania led, not simply to such absurdities as bin

Laden reportedly selling undetonated Tomahawk cruise missiles to China for $10 million, but to the Saudi's apotheosis as the jihadist champion who had taken on the Great Satan and prevailed. As Lawrence Wright writes, "When bin Laden's exhilarated voice came crackling across a radio transmission [after a failed cruise missile attack on his Afghan headquarters]–'By the grace of God, I am alive!'–the forces of anti-Americanism had found their champion. Those Muslims who had objected to the slaughter of innocents in the embassies in East Africa were cowed by the popular support for this man whose defiance of America now seemed blessed by divine favor. Even in Kenya and Tanzania, the two countries that had suffered most from al-Qaeda's attacks, children would be spotted wearing bin-Laden T-shirts."[3] Then came the next step, on October 12, 2000.

The guided missile destroyer USS *Cole* had been named for a Marine Medal of Honor winner at Iwo Jima; an expression of American technological prowess with a sharp, clipperlike profile, *Cole* had cost the taxpayers of the United States a billion dollars. Like her sisters on a memorable morning long ago and far away in Hawaii, *Cole*, moored at a refueling buoy in the harbor of Aden, seemed invulnerable; her AEGIS radar-and-targeting system could track attacking missiles and planes as far as two hundred miles away. Lawrence Wright picks up the story:

At 11:15 a.m., as the *Cole* was preparing to get under way, a fiberglass fishing boat approached its massive prey. Some of the sailors were standing watch, but many were below decks or waiting in the chow line. Two men brought the tiny skiff to a halt amidships, smiled and waved, then stood at attention. The symbolism and the asymmetry of this moment were exactly what bin Laden had dreamed of. "The destroyer represented the capital of the West," he said, "and the small boat represented Muhammad."

The shock wave of the enormous explosion in the harbor knocked over cars onshore. Two miles away, people thought there was an earthquake ...

A fireball rose from the waterline and swallowed a sailor who had leaned over the rail to see what the men in the little boat were up to. The blast opened a hole forty feet by forty feet in the port side of the ship, tearing apart sailors who were waiting for lunch. Seventeen of them perished, and thirty-nine were wounded. Several of the sailors swam through the blast hole to escape the flames. The great modern man-of-war was gaping open like a gutted animal.[4]

The Clinton administration—disempowered by scandal, fighting an election campaign, and eager to close a deal between Israel and the Palestinians in its last weeks in office—did nothing. The countersymbol to bin Laden's jihadists-versus-Leviathan scenario in the harbor at Aden would be Secretary of State Madeleine Albright, running down the driveway at Camp David, in a desperate attempt to keep Yasser Arafat at the presidential retreat and negotiating. The al-Qaeda mastermind, not surprisingly, was unimpressed.

Indeed, he was further provoked. For when the United States failed to respond to the attack on the *Cole* in such a way as to ignite the war in Afghanistan in which bin Laden hoped to trap the Americans (as, according to his own mythology, he had trapped the Soviets), he decided that, according to his understanding of the dynamics of history, something else was required: as Lawrence Wright puts it, "he would have to create an irresistible outrage."[5] The result was a vast hole in the ground in lower Manhattan, the loss of almost three thousand lives, an economic cost of billions of dollars, the laceration of the American national psyche, and a poisoning of American politics unseen since the sixties.

Osama bin Laden, in other words, *wanted* war, as he had tried to make clear in his 1996 "Declaration of War Against America," issued from a cave in Afghanistan.[6] To use an overused verb in the precise and correct sense, he *needed* war, for the fulfillment of his purposes. And in that conviction, Osama bin Laden was not, and is not, alone.

To understand that jihadists read history in a distinctive way leads to several other sublessons:

(1) As Prime Minister Tony Blair insisted in his September 2006 address to the British Labour Party's annual conference, "This terrorism isn't our fault," and "until we shake ourselves free of the wretched capitulation to the propaganda of the enemy, that somehow we are the ones responsible," we will not prevail. Or, as Fouad Ajami has written, "It was not an isolated band of young men who came America's way on 9/11. They emerged out of the Arab world's dominant culture and malignancies."[7] Those malignancies have many sources; one of those sources is defective theology, and we deny that at our peril.

(2) Jihadism is not caused by poverty. Sayyid Qutb, as noted previously, sailed to the United States in a first-class cabin in the days when that kind of transportation was the embodiment of luxury. The nineteen death cultists of 9/11 were middle class and well educated. It is true that some jihadists claim to act in the name of the "wretched of the earth." But as Walter Laqueur points out, "in the forty-nine countries currently designated by the United Nations as the least developed hardly any terrorist activity occurs . . . [Even] in the Sudan . . . it was not the native Sudanese element that played the main [terrorist] role but foreign terrorists who were hiding in the country and using it as a training ground."[8]

Poverty, in and of itself, doesn't turn men and women into jihadists. By the same token, however,

Laqueur notes that "demographic growth and the incapacity of the Arab governments to find jobs for young people leaving the schools and graduating from the universities" has "contributed to the terrorist potential in the Arab world."[9] Potential terrorists become terrorists in reality, however, when grim life prospects caused by sclerotic and corrupt politics meet an apocalyptic ideology of salvation via the jihadist cult of death.

(3) Jihadism isn't caused by the fact of the State of Israel. Israel is, for jihadists, the excuse, not the reason; or, as Fouad Ajami writes, Israel is "the deadliest of all Arab alibis" in a political culture formed in part by an ideology of victimhood.[10] Jihadists do not hate the West because of Israel, they hate Israel because it is part of the West—hence, that standard jihadist trope, "Zionist-Crusaders," which bespeaks a kind of global struggle, which in turn explains why the withdrawal of U.S. troops from Saudi Arabia did not satisfy Osama bin Laden and other jihadists.

The indictment of Israel is also, as Walter Laqueur notes (and one suspects the Lebanese-born Ajami would agree), an example of "the time-honored tradition in the Muslim world to put most or all of the blame [for] its failures on foreigners rather than on their own shortcomings." This disinclination "to engage in self-criticism" has one of its roots in Islamic supersessionism—reasons for Muslim failure *cannot* be the result of any deficiencies in God's final revelation—and helps explain why the fact and the success of Israel seem to so many Muslims to be the result of a vast global conspiracy against them.[11]

It is thus a great folly to think that jihadism and the terrorism it underwrites can be understood in terms drawn primarily from the patois of the therapeutic society, as if jihadist terrorism were some levantine form of psychiatric aberration. Within their own theological frame of reference and the reading of history it warrants, jihadists are not crazy. They make, to themselves, a terrible kind of sense.

It is an even greater folly not to take jihadist leaders like Hezbollah's Hassan Nasrallah with great seriousness when they pass sentence: "Let the entire world hear me. Our hostility to the Great Satan [the United States] is absolute. . . . Regardless of how the world has changed after 11 September, 'Death to America' will remain our reverberating and powerful slogan: 'Death to America.'"[12]

Hassan Nasrallah was not speaking metaphorically.

LESSON 6. It is not "Islamophobic" to note the historical connection between conquest and Muslim expansion, or between contemporary jihadism and terrorism. Truth-telling is the essential prerequisite to genuine interreligious dialogue, which can only be based on the claims of reason.

Alain Besançon concludes his analysis of the differences between Judaism and Christianity, on the one hand, and Islam, on the other, with this trenchant observation:

> Efforts to engage in "dialogue" with Muslims have been set on a mistaken course. The early Church fathers deemed the works of Virgil and Plato a *preparatio evangelica*–preparation for the Gospel, for the truth of Christianity. The Qur'an is neither a preparation for biblical religion nor a retroactive endorsement of it. In approaching Muslims, self-respecting Christians and others would do better to rely on

what remains within Islam of natural religion—and of religious virtue—and to take into
account the common humanity that Muslims
share with all people everywhere.[1]

Pope Benedict XVI's Regensburg Lecture in September 2006 took a similar tack.[2] At Regensburg, the
Pope identified the deepest theological source of jihadist ideology—its defective concept of God—and
gave the world an interreligious and ecumenical vocabulary by which Muslims, Christians, Jews, adherents of other world religions, and nonbelievers
can engage in a genuine conversation about the
threat posed to the human future by jihadism: the
vocabulary of rationality and irrationality.

Widely criticized at the time as an intemperate
and offensive assault on Muslim sensibilities, Benedict's Regensburg Lecture in fact led, within a
month, to one of the few hopeful events of 2006: the
"Open Letter to Pope Benedict XVI" originally signed
by thirty-eight prominent Islamic leaders from
across the globe.[3] In that letter, these Muslim leaders
welcomed the Pope's call for an intellectually serious
encounter between Muslims and Christians; rejected the jihadists' interpretations of "jihad" as an
obligatory holy war of conquest, to be waged until
Allah's sovereignty is acknowledged by the entire
world; and condemned those "who have disregarded
a long and well-established tradition in favor of
utopian dreams where the end justifies the means,"

writing that those who had done this "have done so of their own accord and without the sanction of God, his Prophet, or the learned tradition." The signatories went on to invite the Pope to a serious theological dialogue on the transcendence of God, and on the relationship of God's nature and attributes to human categories of understanding. They also suggested that, in the mainstream Islamic tradition, God cannot command the irrational—like the murder of innocents.[4]

The "Open Letter" was hardly flawless. It distorted history at points, and it contained no mechanism for specific follow-up. Jihadist murderers, while condemned, were not condemned by name, nor did the "Open Letter" address the pathological anti-Semitism that infects too much of the Islamic world. So there is much that needs further discussion. Yet it is not without interest that this statement—which despite its shortcomings was still the most forthcoming from senior Muslim leaders in living memory—followed a robust and courageous critique of the theological roots of jihadism, not the exchange of banalities and pleasantries that too often characterizes interreligious dialogue. Surely there are lessons here for the future.

The first is that the western media acquiescence to Muslim complaints about western, American, Christian, or papal "Islamophobia" should stop. It is not "Islamophobic" for the Pope, or anyone else, to pray in the presence of Muslims, to defend religious freedom, or to condemn violence perpetrated in the name of God—suggestions variously made by National Public Radio, the *New York Times*, the Associated Press, and the New York *Daily News* during Benedict XVI's December 2006 visit to Turkey. It would also be helpful if the western press—and particularly that part of the western press that reaches the Islamic world, like CNN and the BBC—would call things by their right names: murderers in Iraq are murderers and terrorists, not insurgents or sectarians; suicide bombers are, in fact, homicide bombers; and so forth.[5]

The Islamic leaders' "Open Letter" also suggests the imperative of a redefined interreligious dialogue. That dialogue would address the question of Islam's ability to assimilate, in a critical way, the achievements of the Enlightenment—a question with which Christianity has been wrestling for centuries and which Islam must now finally engage. This was precisely the focus of interreligious dialogue Benedict XVI proposed in his Christmas 2006 address to the Roman Curia, the central administrative apparatus of the Catholic Church. In it, the Pope made four crucial points.

First, history itself has put before the Islamic world the "urgent task" of finding a way to come to grips with the intellectual and institutional achievements of the Enlightenment: the Muslim world can no longer live as if the Enlightenment, in both its achievements and its flaws, had not happened. Second, this necessary Islamic encounter with Enlightenment thought and the institutions of governance that grew out of Enlightenment political theory requires separating the wheat from the chaff: the skepticism and relativism that characterize one stream of Enlightenment thought need not (and indeed should not) be accepted; yet one can (and must) make distinctions and accept the ideas that the Enlightenment got right—for example, religious freedom, understood as an inalienable human right to be acknowledged and protected by government—even as one rejects the ideas of which the Enlightenment made a hash (for example, the idea of God). Third, this process of coming to grips with the complex heritage and continuing momentum of the Enlightenment is an ongoing one. As the experience of the Catholic Church has demonstrated in recent decades, however, an ancient religious tradition can appropriate certain aspects of Enlightenment thought, and can come to appreciate the institutions of freedom that emerged from the Enlightenment, without compromising in a fundamental way its own core theological commitments—indeed, the experience of the Catholic Church on the question of religious freedom and the institutional separation of Church and state shows that a serious, critical engagement with Enlightenment ideas and institutions can lead a religious community to a revivification of classic theological concepts that may have lain dormant for a long period of time, and thus to a genuine development of religious understanding. Fourth, it is precisely on this ground–the ground where faith meets reason–that interreligious dialogue should be constructed.[6]

All of which is to say that the interreligious dialogue of the future should focus on helping those Muslims willing to do so to explore the possibility of an Islamic case for religious tolerance, social pluralism, and civil society–even as Islam's interlocutors (among Christians, Jews, and others, including nonbelievers) open themselves to the possibility that the Islamic critique of certain aspects of modern culture is not without merit.[7]

Some will say that such an Islamic development of doctrine cannot happen: that the deep theological structures of Islamic self-understanding identified above make any fruitful encounter with the institutional achievements of the Enlightenment (let alone the Enlightenment's intellecutal accomplishments) so unlikely as to be virtually impossible. No one should gainsay the difficulties involved here. Yet Bernard Lewis suggests that what is often seen today–especially by European foreign ministries and the U.S. Department of State–as a natural affinity between Islamic societies and authoritarianism is in fact the product of the past two centuries.

Traditional Muslim societies, Lewis suggests, were characterized by forces that "limited the autocracy of the ruler," including such "established orders" as "the bazaar merchants, the scribes, the guilds, the country gentry, the military establishment, the religious establishment, and so on." The leaders of these powerful groups were not appointed by the state; they arose from within the groups themselves, and no wise ruler could afford to make major decisions without consulting them. This was not "democracy as we currently use that word," Lewis concedes, but neither was it autocracy or even authoritarianism; it was a distinct form of "limited, responsible government." And it was ended, first by the forced modernization imposed by state authority in the Arab Islamic world in the nineteenth century, and then by the Arab Islamic experience of the mid-twentieth century, which Lewis sketches in these trenchant terms:

> In the year 1940, the government of France surrendered to the Axis and formed a collaborationist government in a place called Vichy. The French colonial empire was, for the most part, beyond the reach of the Nazis, which means that the governors of the French colonies had a free choice: to stay with Vichy or to join Charles de Gaulle, who had set up a Free French Committee in London. The overwhelming majority chose Vichy, which meant that Syria-Lebanon—a French-mandated territory in the heart of the Arab East—was now wide open to the Nazis.
>
> The governor and his high officials in the administration in Syria-Lebanon took their

orders from Vichy, which in turn took orders
from Berlin. The Nazis moved in, made a tremendous propaganda effort, and were even
able to move from Syria eastwards into Iraq
and for a while set up a pro-Nazi, fascist
regime. It was in this period that political par-
ties were formed that were the nucleus of
what later became the Baath Party. The Western Allies eventually drove the Nazis out of the
Middle East and suppressed these organizations. But the war ended in 1945 and the Allies
left. A few years later the Soviets moved in, established an immensely powerful presence in
Egypt, Syria, Iraq, and various other countries,
and introduced Soviet-style political practice.
The adaptation from the Nazi model to the
communist model was very simple and easy,
requiring only a few minor adjustments, and
it proceeded pretty well. That is the origin of
the Baath Party and of the kind of governments that we have been confronting in the
Middle East in recent years. That, as I would
again repeat and emphasize, has nothing
whatever to do with the traditional Arab or Islamic past.[8]

The development of those elements of pluralism
identified in Lewis's depiction of the Islamic past
into a future akin to what the West refers to as "civil
society" is a project that Islamic reformers must pur-

sue with great urgency, given the threat posed by global jihadism. It is often said that "Islam needs a Reformation"—that the world awaits an "Islamic Luther" or an "Islamic Calvin." This is a bit too easy, however, in terms of its close identification of the Reformation with the emergence of free societies in the West, and in its understanding of what ails politicized Islam. Rather than an Islamic Luther, Islamic reformers might better look toward the possibility of an Islamic Leo XIII: toward the possibility of a religious leader who reaches back into the deeper philosophical resources of his tradition in order to broker a critical engagement with Enlightenment political thought, and to shape his tradition's encounter with the economic and political institutions of modernity.

Pope Leo XIII was not the father of the modern social doctrine of the Catholic Church because he fostered a rupture with tradition (*pace* Luther or Calvin). Rather, Leo understood that the highly politicized idea of "tradition" that prevailed in much of nineteenth-century Catholicism was not, in fact, traditional, and that the political arrangements it favored—such as the use of state power and authority to enforce the truth claims of the Church—were not the only possible conclusion to be drawn from core Catholic theological premises. Leo XIII's retrieval of authentic Thomistic philosophy as a tool of social analysis led to a remarkable, evolutionary development of social doctrine in the Catholic Church, and eventually to the Second Vatican Council's historic

Declaration on Religious Freedom, a high-water mark in the disentanglement of the Church from state power–the disentanglement of *sacerdotium* from *regnum*. That process of retrieval and development, as distinct from rupture and revolution, is a model that can be recommended to genuine Islamic reformers today. Such an approach, emphasizing the capacity of reason to get at the truth of things, also holds out the possibility of an interreligious dialogue that is more than an exchange of either platitudes or shibboleths.

Non-Muslims can play no significant role in the intra-Islamic struggle to come to grips with Enlightenment ideas and free political institutions, for that struggle must be resolved, finally, in terms of Islamic premises. But non-Muslims can, just possibly, help shape the contours of that struggle from outside.

They can do so by not giving most-favored-dialogue-partner status to those establishment Muslim religious authorities who still find it impossible to condemn jihadism. A Muslim religious leader who will not condemn suicide/homicide bombing, publicly and with the perpetrators condemned by name, is not a religious leader with whom reasonable people can be in serious conversation. Public condemnation of jihadism and jihadists ought to be the admission ticket required of any Islamic religious leader or scholar who seeks dialogue with western religious or intellectual institutions, and with western political and religious leaders. And that requires prudence on the part of westerners, who

may not be aware that what a prominent Islamic figure says on media being broadcast to the English-
speaking world is sometimes not the same thing as
what he says on al-Jazeera. It should go without saying that anti-Semites and Holocaust deniers are like-
wise disqualified as dialogue partners.[9]

Non-Muslims can also help shape the terrain of
the intra-Islamic struggle by working with those
Muslim scholars, religious leaders, and activists who
are trying to revive the tradition of reason in Islam. If
Islam insists that its faith is post-Judeo-Christian, in
the sense that the revelations of the one true God to
the People of Israel and in Jesus Christ have been
completely superseded by the revelation to Muhammad (and in that sense, only Muslims fully grasp
whatever truths remain from prior revelations), then
there is little ground for theological dialogue, strictly
speaking. That theological dialogue may come in
time—perhaps centuries of time. At the moment,
however, the important thing would seem to be to
concentrate on working at such common borders as
exist between us: and the defense of reason against
both jihadists and those postmodernists who deny
the human capacity to know the truth of anything
with certainty could be one such borderland meeting
place, and an important one at that.

If, for example, Jews, Christians, Muslims, and
agnostics (as well as Hindus, Buddhists, and adherents of other religions) could agree that there are
certain moral truths "built into" the world, built into

us, and built into the dynamics of human striving—moral truths that we can know, by careful reflection, to be true—then we would have the first building blocks of a philosophical foundation on which to construct, together, free and just societies that respect religious conviction. We would have, in other words, a rational, interreligious "grammar" and vocabulary with which to engage each other on questions of what is, in fact, the meaning of freedom, justice, and other aspects of the good.

Winston Churchill, a man who did not shrink from fighting when necessary, famously said that "jaw, jaw is better than war, war." Unfortunately, much of what passes for "jaw, jaw" in contemporary interreligious dialogue is, in truth, "blah, blah": in part, because of the political correctness of western dialogue partners, but, at a deeper level, because the dialogue partners have not yet developed a grammar that turns noise (or banality, which amounts to the same thing) into conversation. The development of such a grammar is not only imperative for genuine interreligious dialogue, although it surely is that. It would also aid the efforts of Islamic reformers in their struggle against the jihadists who, they believe, have hijacked Islam—yet who have, in the process, made jihadism perhaps the most dynamic force in the contemporary Islamic world.

LESSON 7. The war against jihadism is a contest for the human future that will endure for generations.

The below-replacement-level birthrates that prevail throughout virtually the entire western world—with the exception of the United States—are another factor in the global struggle for the human future that is being contested with jihadism. As columnist and intellectual provocateur Mark Steyn puts it, based on present demographic trends, "the Belgian climate-change lobbyist will [soon] be on the endangered species list with the Himalayan snow leopard." Given parallels to Belgium in the Netherlands, France, Spain, and elsewhere, the new demographics of depopulation have already changed the political landscape of western Europe.[1]

Yet Steyn notes that birthrates are already declining in some Islamic countries, such that the jihadists' demographic advantage, which has played a role in contemporary jihadism's success, will eventually decrease as well. So the historical window for the achievement of the jihadists' most ambitious goals will likely begin to close in, perhaps, twenty-five years or so. Or, to put it another way, the jihadists, from their perspective, have a generation or two to get the job done. The demographics of the Islamic world, coupled with the longer-term resonance of the passions unleashed by jihadist ideology and distorted religious conviction, thus suggest that the current phase of the contest with jihadism for the human future will last at least two or three generations.

Recognizing that, we can also recognize both the truth and the false comfort of the oft-repeated statement that the overwhelming majority of Muslims are not terrorists or jihadists. As Walter Laqueur writes, "It has been endlessly repeated that the majority of Muslims want to live in peace with their neighbors, a statement that is as correct as it is irrelevant. The believers in jihad are a minority, but they can count on a substantial periphery of sympathizers, more than sufficient to sustain long campaigns of terrorism."[2] Shortening that duration requires a recognition that the pattern Laqueur describes— jihadist core surrounded by sympathetic periphery— exists, not only in the Middle East, but throughout western Europe, in Canada, and in the United States. This, in turn, suggests that western countries must rid themselves of multiculturalist delusions and take the assimilation of immigrants much more seriously than has been the case in recent decades.

"Assimilation," in this instance, means assimilation to the basic norms of civil society on which the free countries of the West are built: respect for pluralism, which includes that respect for others' convictions that makes civil engagement with those who are "other" possible; respect for the rule of law, understood as those civil and criminal laws duly adopted by the people or their legitimate representatives; a commitment to the method of persuasion in political life and a rejection of the methods of coercion (including, of course, violent coercion). Bringing immigrants from outside the civilizational orbit of the West to an appreciation of, respect for, and commitment to these civil society norms must be the task of civic education, which is a crucial component of immigrant assimilation. Democratic citizens are made, not born. "Making citizens" is difficult enough in itself; the difficulties are compounded when it is thought that efforts to "make citizens" are either unnecessary, or an offense against others' culture.

This is, indeed, a long war. It is important that we understand that, acknowledge it politically, gird ourselves for it economically, educate our societies for it, and plan both strategy and tactics accordingly.

Which brings us to the subject of realism.

PART TWO

RETHINKING

REALISM

LESSON 8. Genuine realism in foreign policy takes wickedness seriously, yet avoids premature closure in its thinking about the possibilities of positive change in world politics.

Understanding the inevitable irony, pathos, and tragedy of history; being alert to the dangers of unintended consequences; maintaining a robust skepticism about schemes of human perfection (especially when politics is the chosen instrument of salvation); cherishing democracy without worshipping it–these elements of the Christian realist sensibility, perhaps most eloquently articulated during the mid-twentieth century by Reinhold Niebuhr, remain essential intellectual grounding for anyone thinking seriously about U.S. foreign policy in the war against jihadism. Yet realism, which is less a comprehensive framework for reflection than a set of intellectual and moral cautions, must always be complemented by a confidence in human creativity's capacity to affect the course of history for the better. Things can be made better, if we have the wit, the will, and the patience for it.

As Dean Acheson said at another moment when history's tectonic plates were shifting, the task that he and Harry Truman faced "only slowly revealed itself. As it did so, it began to appear as just a little bit less formidable than that described in the first chapter of Genesis. That was to create a world out of chaos."[1] Our task today is not dissimilar. In carrying it out, we would do well to remember the counsel of the late public philosopher Charles Frankel: "The heart of the policy-making process . . . is not the *finding* of a national interest already perfectly known and understood. It is the *determining* of that interest: the reassessment of the nation's resources, needs, commitments, traditions, and political and cultural horizons—in short, its calendar of values."[2]

Efforts to accelerate change in the Arab Islamic world by the administration of George W. Bush were shaped by a realistic assessment of the situation after 9/11. As Fouad Ajami notes, the "custodians of American power were under great pressure to force history's pace."[3] To attempt to accelerate the transition to responsible and responsive government in the Middle East was neither an exercise in cowboy apocalypticism nor in Wilsonian romanticism. It was a *realistic* objective, given an unacceptable status quo that was inherently unstable; that was unstable because it was corrupt; and that was producing terrorists and jihadists determined to challenge those corruptions.

Oddly enough, the true idealists here are those

who imagined that the "custodians of American power"—who, for better and for worse, exercise a large responsibility for the creation and maintenance of world order in a disorderly world—could continue to manage "stability" by finding, aiding, abetting, and bribing "our bastards" in a Middle East the majority of whose people were denied the economic benefits of its wealth, a region seething with resentment over political corruption and repression and increasingly influenced by the siren song of religiously warranted calls to self-sacrifice and vengeance. Idealism of this sort—the idealism of the unshakable status quo, if you will—misreads things as they are and fails to imagine things as they could be. Genuine realism takes the world as it is; but it does not leave the world as it is, especially when doing so becomes suicidal.

Thus a U.S. foreign policy fit to meet the challenge of jihadism will not mistake cynicism and a lack of imagination for "realism," just as it will not dismiss prudent efforts to change the status quo as vapid and dangerous idealism. The lesson of the 1930s remains salient here: sometimes, things can get very much worse when the custodians of order mistake brittleness for "order" or miss the revolutionary character of those they imagine can be appeased. The diplomacy of preemptive appeasement is a confession of fecklessness. It is also a prescription for disaster, as irresponsible procrastination ultimately leads to dire consequences.

LESSON 9. In the war against jihadism, the political objective in the Middle East and throughout the Islamic world is the evolution of responsible and responsive government, which will take different forms given different historical and cultural circumstances.

Bernard Lewis is, as usual, a wise guide here. As he wrote in 2006,

> There is a view sometimes expressed that "democracy" means the system of government evolved by the English-speaking peoples. Any departure from that is either a crime to be punished or a disease to be cured. I beg to differ from that point of view. Different societies develop different ways of conducting their affairs, and they do not need to resemble ours. And let us remember, after all, that American democracy after the War of Independence was compatible with slavery for three-quarters of a century and with the disenfranchisement of

women for longer than that. Democracy is not born like the Phoenix. It comes in stages, and the stages and processes of development will differ from country to country, from society to society. The French cherish the curious illusion that they invented democracy, but since the great revolution of 1789 they have had two monarchies, two empires, two dictatorships, and at the last count, five republics. And I'm not sure that they've got it right yet.[1]

Professor Lewis's cautions are important in themselves; so are his convictions, previously noted, that "there are elements in Islamic society which could well be conducive" to self-government, and that "developing free institutions—along their lines, not ours—is possible" in Islamic countries. Together, these ideas form an important barrier against premature closure in thinking through the possibilities of an evolving world order. They are also a useful prelude to reflection on the situation in Iraq since 2003. For Iraq was and is, inevitably and crucially, a painful test case for the claim that responsible and responsive government can be built on Islamic cultural foundations. The drama of Iraq will continue to unfold for years, perhaps decades. Understanding that is yet another facet of realism rightly understood. So is recognizing that people who use children as decoys for car bombs are people whose actions are going to be very difficult to predict, and to control.

Still, four years after an American-led coalition invaded Iraq to enforce resolutions the United Nations was unwilling and unable to enforce on its own and to liberate the Iraqi people from the cruel despotism of Saddam Hussein, certain lessons can be drawn.

The primary failure of American policy planning in Iraq was neatly summarized by the *New York Times*'s Michael Gordon and General Bernard Trainor: "What was missing was a comprehensive blueprint to administer and restore Iraq after Saddam was deposed, and identification of the U.S. organizations that would be installed in Baghdad to carry it out."[2] That lack of a strategic blueprint for post-Saddam Iraq reflected, even as it led to, other errors:

(1) American analysts and U.S. policy makers miscalculated the degree to which post-Saddam Iraq would quickly become a battlefield in the wider war against jihadism—which, in Iraq, unleashed a series of bloody events that have made the political stabilization of the country far more difficult. In *The Foreigner's Gift*, Fouad Ajami writes that the quick collapse of a Saddamist regime that had cowed much of the Middle East exposed the "false world" in which Arabs had been living: a world characterized by that distinctive "Arab mix of victimology and wrath" that had defined the Middle East's politics for decades. Such exposure was intolerable: to the remaining Baathists in Iraq, many of whom might have been expected to have been killed in the major combat phase

of the war, but who quickly folded and went—with their weapons—to ground; to the Baathists in Syria; to the forces of the status quo among the Arab leadership; to the apocalyptics in Tehran; and to jihadists everywhere. And so each of them, in their several ways, worked as interlocking parts of a perfect storm to impede the "foreigner's gift" to Iraq of political freedom and the forms of democratic self-government.

Had the United States recognized that the "links" between Iraq and jihadist terrorism were of a different sort than the conspiracies for which western intelligence agencies were searching—had we understood that, in the jihadists' worldview, a democratic Iraq, created by American military and economic power linked to Iraqi people power, was intolerable—then American policy makers might have understood that the jihadists would bend every effort to turn Iraq into what Ajami calls a "devil's playground," the porous borders of which "were a magnet for jihadists looking for a field of battle"—Jordanians, Syrians, Lebanese, Saudis, Palestinians, Iranians, all of whom grasped the fact that, if America were to succeed in Iraq, and Iraq to succeed as a modern Islamic society, their various dreams would be dealt a major, perhaps lethal, blow. On this field of battle, the jihadists were de facto allies of other miscreants: the Syrian government, the Iranian government, and the government of the Palestinian Authority, none of whose behavior toward Iraq was seriously challenged by the forces of so-called Arab moderation (Egypt, Jordan, Saudi Arabia)—who were strikingly unconcerned with the slaughter of Muslims by fellow Muslims—or by the United States and its allies.[5]

In sum, American analysts and policy makers did not grasp quickly enough that major combat in Iraq had only (to quote Robert Kaplan) "shaped the battlefield" for what was coming next—a counter-insurgency war against Baathist and Iraqi military diehards and jihadists (in which America's information-technology military advantage would be gravely weakened), followed by (and in some respects coterminous with) a sectarian conflict between Iraqi Sunni and Iraqi Shia dominated by terrorist tactics.[4] Even though executing the Cobra II war plan had required a lot of improvisation along the road to Baghdad and in the capture of Baghdad itself, the United States was reasonably well prepared for the first Iraq war: the war to depose Saddam Hussein and create the possibility of responsible Iraqi government. America was prepared neither militarily, nor intellectually, nor politically for the three wars that followed—the war against the remaining Iraqi Baathists and their allies; the war against Abu Mussab al-Zarqawi of "Al-Qaeda in Iraq" and other jihadists; and the war between Shia and Sunni that exploded in earnest after the February 2006 bombing of the Shia shrine of the Golden Mosque in Samarra (which seems to have been an al-Qaeda operation). American policy planners were unprepared for Iraq's immediate ungovernability following major combat; and American policy makers remained tone deaf for too long to the religious dimensions of the fourth war in Iraq, which too many Iraqis in fact welcomed.

(2) American analysts and policy makers badly miscalculated the degree of damage done to the fabric of Iraqi civil society by more than twenty-five years of Baathist totalitarianism. This, in turn, led to underestimating seriously the difficulties of accelerating a return to a functioning economy after the overthrow of the Saddam Hussein regime. As Robert Kaplan writes, describing the situation as he experienced it in the spring of 2004:

> The social and cultural refuse created by the [Baathist] regime was everywhere, overwhelming the American authorities. While clichés abounded about the talent of the Iraqi people and their ability to quickly build a vibrant capitalist society, officers of the 82nd Airborne who had been [in Iraq] for months told another, more familiar story: of how Iraqis, like their Syrian neighbors, had in recent decades not experienced Western capitalism so much as a diseased variant of it, in which you couldn't even open a restaurant or a shop without having connections to the regime. Above the level of the street vendor, in other words, capitalism [in Iraq] would have to be learned from scratch.[5]

The social incapacities induced by Saddam Hussein's totalitarianism intersected with the depredations to civil society caused by the wider Arab Islamic culture of "false redeemers and pretenders" (as Fouad Ajami describes it) to make the formation of a rudimentary democratic political culture in Iraq extremely difficult. That problem was compounded, in turn, by the capacity of al-Jazeera and other new-technology Arab-language media to spread lies; as Ajami writes in *The Foreigner's Gift*, "the new technology was put at the service of an old and stubborn refusal to face and name things as they are."[6]

(3) Inadequate financial and human resources were allocated for post-Saddam reconstruction in Iraq. As Max Boot writes in *War Made New*,

> A dangerous [post-Saddam] security vacuum [was exacerbated by a] . . . lack of reconstruction assistance. Only $2.5 billion had been budgeted initially to rebuild Iraq, an amount that would prove grossly inadequate, given the dilapidated condition in which Saddam Hussein's misrule and a decade of sanctions had left the country and especially its oil industry. (Administration officials would later claim that they had no idea in advance of how run-down everything was, but private experts had foreseen the need for at least $25 billion to $100 billion in reconstruction aid). In November 2003 Congress voted $18.4 billion in further

aid for Afghanistan and Iraq, but the money had to flow through so many bureaucratic brooks and eddies that only a trickle reached its ultimate destination. As of December 2004, just $2 billion had been spent in Iraq–and much of that went for security and overhead costs incurred by American contractors.[7]

Here, as in the days before 9/11, the American intelligence community did not provide policy makers and planners what they needed, for American intelligence failed to grasp just how much damage had been done to Iraq's infrastructure by the Gulf War, and by the combination of sanctions-driven economic stagnation and Saddam Hussein's perverse priorities in the 1990s.

To make matters worse, there was, from the beginning, a mind-boggling lack of bureaucratic coordination among American agencies responsible for reconstruction efforts in Iraq. Struggles between the Department of Defense and the Department of State over which of the two would be the lead agency in postwar Iraq–struggles that the White House could have resolved, but did not–exacerbated the lack of interagency coordination. According to Gordon and Trainor, Secretary of Defense Donald Rumsfeld distrusted the State Department's capacity to lead and coordinate and feared that the bureaucratic sluggishness at Foggy Bottom would end up balkanizing Iraq. Rumsfeld may also have believed that Defense could restore order in Iraq as efficiently as the U.S. military and its allies had defeated Saddam's army. The leadership vacuum caused by this bureaucratic squabbling made it even more difficult to recognize that the original levels of reconstruction aid anticipated were gravely deficient. The Bush administration did not grasp quickly enough that "money is ammunition"–a lesson about fighting a postliberation counterinsurgency war that General David Petraeus, who would become field commander in Iraq in early 2007, had identified a year and a half previously.[8]

Bush administration officials may, as Gordon and Trainor suggest, have brought a settled skepticism about "nation building" to their thinking about post-Saddam Iraq. But *state* building was in fact the responsibility the United States had taken on as an unavoidable implication of the judgment–correct, in my view–that regime change in Iraq was imperative. Strengthening the severely attenuated sinews of Iraq civil society and building the rudiments of democratic self-governance amidst massive economic dislocations (and bad economic habits) were essential objectives of any coherent and comprehensive coalition strategy for the new Iraq. All of this should have been thought through more carefully before March 2003–not to mention when it became unmistakably clear a year after the post–"major combat" phase of the Iraq Wars.[9]

(4) American policy makers failed to devise an ef-

fective hearts-and-minds strategy for post-Saddam Iraq. After dominating the information dimensions of the first of the four Iraq Wars (the war against the Saddam Hussein regime), the United States too often left the information field to sources of misinformation and disinformation like al-Jazeera, with serious strategic consequences. Max Boot describes the deleterious effects of this default on the first battle for Fallujah in April 2004, a crucial moment in the second of the four Iraq Wars:

> On April 4, 2004, two Marine battalions launched an assault on Fallujah. Five days later, while Marines were still battling their way into the city, the offensive was suspended because of inflammatory media coverage, primarily on the Arabic satellite news channel al-Jazeera, which claimed that Marines were deliberately targeting mosques and civilians. [Coalition Provisional Authority head Paul] Bremer, [General John] Abizaid, and other senior officials feared that, if the operation continued, support for the U.S. would crumble throughout the country. . . .
>
> In Fallujah, negative news coverage succeeded in doing what Saddam Hussein's military had failed to do: it stopped the mighty U.S. military in its tracks. As Lieutenant General James Conway, commander of the 1st Marine

Expeditionary Force, put it, "Al-Jazeera kicked
our butts." The Marines had to leave Fallujah,
handing the insurgents their most notable victory.[10]

Al-Jazeera lied; the lies were believed, in a culture all too accustomed to believing lies; the political environment changed, for the worse. That
disinformation-driven failure in Fallujah was itself a
blow to building responsible government in Iraq. It
would only be reversed months later at the cost of
numerous American and Iraqi casualties.

This broad inventory does not exhaust the cata-
logue of American misapprehensions and failures in
Iraq—and the mistakes began early. To take but
two crucial examples: The looting and the general
breakdown of public order that followed the collapse
of the Saddam Hussein regime should have been met
with a far firmer response. The virtual disappearance of Iraq's borders, the openness of which
permitted, indeed encouraged, large numbers of
jihadists to enter the country, is an ongoing problem
that began very early in the post–major combat
phase and cannot be solved by Predator drones
alone. Unwilling to appear as anything other than
liberators, however, and lacking the troops to main-
tain public order and patrol the borders, the U.S.-led
coalition let the window of opportunity they had
opened by the swiftness of their military victory in
March–April 2003 close.

Others share a measure of blame here. Where were America's allies, not to mention the "international community," when large numbers of troops for border security and massive funds for economic reconstruction were required? Too many countries, it seems, were more interested in "teaching the United States a lesson" than in the people of Iraq, or in the effects of an Iraqi debacle on the war against jihadism. That being said, and meant, the failures of others should not diminish the degree of responsibility to be borne by the United States—or the imperatives of America learning from its postliberation mistakes in Iraq. It was the United States (to be sure, supported by Great Britain, Australia, Poland, and others) that had taken the decision to depose the Saddam Hussein regime; the United States was in charge; and the United States had failed, prior to the invasion, to think through and plan for the worst-case scenarios, several of which were to unfold with savage rapidity.

When British historian Niall Ferguson argued in 2004 that the United States lacked an imperial play-book but badly needed one, he was, it should now be clear, on to something important. In retrospect, it seems astonishing that the relevant governmental and intellectual circles gave so little thought to the lessons that might have been learned from the post-totalitarian experiences of various countries in central and eastern Europe after the Cold War—lessons that could have been applied, with appropriate adjustments for the different cultural circumstances, to post-totalitarian Iraq. But doing that would have required the United States to take a break from its 1990s holiday from history. And that neither the American people nor the U.S. government was prepared to do.

The immense difficulties of post-Baathist political transition in Iraq should not lead to a false realism of premature closure, however. Nor should those difficulties blind us to the fact that, as Bernard Lewis has written, "The war against terror and the quest for freedom are inextricably linked, and neither can succeed without the other." Moreover, and without gainsaying the difficulties involved, our most distinguished scholar of Islamic history concludes that the study of that history, and of the complex Muslim literature on politics, finally encourages us to think that, in the Islamic world, "it may well be possible to develop democratic institutions—not necessarily in our Western definition of that much misused term, but in one deriving from their own history and culture and ensuring, in their own way, limited government under law, consultation and openness, in a civilized and humane society. There is enough in the traditional culture of Islam on the one hand and the modern experience of the Muslim peoples on the other to provide the basis for an advance toward freedom in the true sense of that word."[11]

Trying, through a variety of instrumentalities, to

support, and perhaps even accelerate, that advance is the realistic course of action.

And that, in turn, suggests that, for the conduct of the war against jihadism, the United States badly needs the equivalent of NSC-68, the famous document drafted by Paul Nitze, under the authority of Secretary of State Dean Acheson, that defined the enemy in the Cold War and the strategy that would be deployed to meet its threat. In the years after World War II, as in the years after the Cold War, Americans seemed eager for a vacation from history. Moreover, the default positions in the relevant governmental departments had not been reset in light of new global realities and the new global responsibilities of the United States had to assume in the wake of the collapse of British imperial power after World War II. NSC-68, as Acheson would later recall, was intended to "so bludgeon the mass mind of 'top government' that not only could the President make a decision but that the decision could be carried out."[12]

The Bush administration attempted something similar to NSC-68 in its National Security Strategy document of 2002 and in President Bush's second inaugural address. NSS-2002 argued (correctly, from a classic just war point of view) that it is sometimes both necessary and morally appropriate to shoot first; the second inaugural address defended the universality of human rights and argued that the advance of the freedom agenda is an essential component of the pursuit of world order. Neither point was, however, connected to the other, nor were those ideas linked explicitly to the threat of jihadism (as NSC-68 had begun with an analysis of the nature of the Soviet threat).

The United States needs the equivalent of an NSC-68 for the twenty-first-century struggle against jihadism, an alternative conception of the human future carried by a messianic creed and advanced by ruthless means. Which, come to think of it, was precisely what Dean Acheson and Paul Nitze were facing in 1950. If they could see clearly and plan prudently then, there is no reason why we cannot do the same now.

LESSON 10. In the war against global jihadism, deterrence strategies are unlikely to be effective, because it is almost impossible to deter those who are committed to their own martyrdom.

To call for a new NSC-68 that does for the twenty-first century what Acheson and Nitze's document did for the late twentieth is not to suggest that their strategy for coping with Soviet power–deterrence–is likely to work in the face of the equally existential threat posed by global jihadism. On the contrary, there is every reason to believe that, given the "logic" that informs jihadist thinking, deterrence strategies are more likely to be ineffective, in part because of the nature of the enemy and in part because jihadists usually perceive efforts to deter them as the kind of weakness that invites attack.

This is perhaps most evident in Iran, where, as Adam Garfinkle notes, eleventh-grade textbooks teach that "in the coming era-ending war against the infidels, Muslims cannot lose: 'Either we all become free, or we will go to the greater freedom which is martyrdom. Either we shall shake one another's hand at the victory of Islam in the world, or all of us will turn to eternal life and martyrdom. In both cases, success and victory are ours.' " As Garfinkle then asks, almost redundantly, "How does one deter people who believe that, who are willing and even eager—from the sound of it—to turn their country and their entire religious sect into a suicide bomb?"[1]

Those who crave martyrdom can rarely be deterred. That is a serious problem for the United States, as 9/11 made unmistakably clear. Those who imagine that their martyrdom will hasten the advent of the messianic age are even less susceptible to deterrence. That is likely to be a grave problem for Israel, and sooner rather than later, as Iran's pursuit of nuclear weapons continues at a furious pace. Israel's immediate problem is also a problem for the United States and for Europe, however, for there is little doubt that an Iranian regime capable of the nuclear incineration of Jerusalem and Tel Aviv would willingly transfer nuclear material to global jihadists, who would thus be empowered to continue the carnage even if (as French president Jacques Chirac delicately put it in January 2007), "Tehran [were] razed to the ground." In the wake of this expression of French sangfroid (which was really insouciance masquerading as another form of crackpot realism), the editors of the *Wall Street Journal* got the point: "We doubt many Israelis will share Mr. Chirac's faith in nuclear deterrence against Islamists who prize

martyrdom."[2] Americans would be wise to be similarly skeptical. From the seizure of American diplomats in Tehran in 1979 through a subsequent
quarter century in which they seized more than a
thousand hostages from dozens of countries, the
Iranian Revolutionary Guards, the shock troops of
Ayatollah Khomeini's revolution, have not hesitated
to violate basic standards of decency and elementary
standards of international public life—and have done
so while the Islamic Republic of Iran is a conven-
tionally armed power. What would they do—and
what would the plausible range of western re-
sponses be—if Iran becomes a nuclear weapons
power? Jacques Chirac, who once threatened the use
of the French nuclear force in retaliation against a
nuclear attack from a state like Iran, seems to think
that the Cold War deterrence strategy of mutual assured destruction works with apocalyptics; the more
prudent course would be to assume that mutual assured destruction is, in this instance, an inducement
rather than a deterrent.[3]

Those who opted for appeasement and deterrence
in the mid-1930s could not say that Adolf Hitler
hadn't warned them: statesmen who cared to look
could find, buried in the turgid prose of *Mein Kampf*,
Hitler's entire program, including German rearma-
ment, the "drive to the East" for *Lebensraum* [living
space], and the slaughter of the European Jews. In
1933, it was a serious mistake to dismiss *Mein
Kampf* as the ravings of a lunatic. It would be a grave

mistake today to think that the mullahs in Iran are simply raving when one of their websites, quoting the Ayatollah Khomeini, declares that "we must get ready to search for . . . liberal democratic civilization in history museums," or when the same website eagerly anticipates the "beautiful and auspicious . . . day when the world is cleansed of deceit and mischief and the government of justice is established throughout the world"—a day we are assured "is nigh," its advent presumably hastened by nuclear devastation. These postings, it should be noted, emanate from the circles surrounding the disciples of Ayatollah Mesbah-Yazdi of Qum, which include Iranian President Mahmoud Ahmadinejad.[4]

It's worth pausing briefly to consider the case of President Ahmadinejad, who embodies a distinctively Shiite form of jihadism. Sunni jihadists like Osama bin Laden, following in the line that runs from Taymiyya and Wahhab to al-Banna and Qutb, seek to establish a new, universal caliphate. Shiite jihadists, like Ahmadinejad, have a somewhat different strategic goal: to hasten the return of a messianic figure, the Twelfth Imam, who will establish, as that website noted above proclaimed, a "world . . . cleansed of deceit and mischief"—in other words, the messianic age. It is true that many of the great world religious have an apocalyptic dimension, a theory of the end time. Shiite apocalypticism as embodied in Ahmadinejad, however, is apocalypticism with a difference.

I remember meeting a group of Christian funda-
mentalists at Masada in Israel in early September
1990. Saddam Hussein had just invaded and occupied Kuwait, and virtually every tourist had left the
Holy Land—except these American apocalyptics,
whose distinctive reading of the Bible led them to
imagine that they had just been given free tickets to
the Battle of Armageddon. Still, their theology did
not compel them to hasten the apocalypse. That
would take place at a time of God's choosing; all they
had to do was read the signs of the times. Ahmadinejad's apocalypticism is qualitatively different: he and
those of his cast of mind believe themselves obli-
gated to do whatever they can to hasten the arrival
of the messianic age—including incinerating Israel,
even if that results in the destruction (or, as they
would say, "martyrdom") of their own country.[5]

Mahmoud Ahmadinejad, who has spoken of the
destruction of the United States and Great Britain as
well as of Israel, is a man whose mind is difficult for
westerners to understand in anything other than psy-
chopathological categories. It is far wiser, however,
to regard him as quite sane—meaning, quite purposeful—within his own theological frame of reference.
He sponsors international conferences dedicated to
promoting the lunatic "history" of Holocaust denial.[6] He supports terrorism, both Shia and Sunni,
throughout the region and likely throughout the
world; Americans undergoing extensive rehabilita-
tion after losing limbs in roadside bomb attacks in

Iraq can, in some cases, rightly consider Ahmadinejad as the cause of their suffering. He lives, as German political scientist Matthias Küntzel writes, in a
"parallel universe in which the reality principle is
ignored . . . a universe in which the laws of reason
have been abolished."[7] That parallel universe, however, is supported by what Ahmadinejad regards,
however mistakenly, as deep theological truths.

What, then, is to be done, if deterrence is not a realistic option, given the nature of this particular
threat from Shiite jihadism? "Regime change" has
gotten a bad name as a policy option, given the difficulties the United States and its allies have experienced in post-Saddam Iraq. It is not easy, however, to
see a way through to safety—for the Iranian people,
for the millions throughout the Holy Land (Jews,
Muslims, Christians, and others) who would be victims of Iranian nuclear weapons, for the West, or for
the cause of world order—without regime change
in Tehran. Iran, conducting its affairs as a normal
nation-state, can be a regional power, a friend of the
West, and a contributor to world economic and cultural life. For so long as the Iranian state is controlled by apocalyptics, however, Iran is a danger to
itself and to the world—as Iranian support for
Hezbollah's destruction of Lebanon and the Iranian
nuclear program, conducted in brazen defiance of
international norms, demonstrate.

Kenneth Timmerman, who has spent years study-

ing the Iranian threat, argued in 2005 against taking
the kinetic route to regime change in Tehran:

> A full scale U.S. military strike on Iran would
> be costly, ineffective, and counterproductive.
> We would probably fail to take out all of Iran's
> hidden nuclear assets. In addition, U.S. intelli-
> gence officials argue in private, we would give
> the regime a winning argument to mobilize
> those citizens who might otherwise support
> pro-democracy forces. Instead, we should em-
> power the pro-democracy forces to change the
> regime. We should do so openly, and as a gov-
> ernment policy. But we should support non-
> governmental organizations, primarily Iranian,
> to do the work.[8]

Former CIA director R. James Woolsey, who has
also been sounding the warning signals about the
Iranian threat for years, agreed with Timmerman's
approach in January 2007 testimony before the
Committee on Foreign Affairs of the U.S. House of
Representatives. Stressing that there are no "easy an-
swers" to the very difficult problem Iran poses,
Woolsey, "convinced that the Iranian regime is fun-
damentally incorrigible," but "not yet ready to propose an all-out use of military force to change the
regime and halt its nuclear program," argued that
"we should opt for trying to bring about, non-

violently, a regime change" by engaging "with the Iranian people, not their oppressors."[9]

Both Timmerman and Woolsey argue that any engagement with the Iranian regime gives it a legitimacy it has demonstrated that it does not deserve, and would be, in any case, read as weakness by President Ahmadinejad and by the mullahs who are in ultimate control of Iranian politics. Late in the day as it may be, the more prudent course, Timmerman and Woolsey suggest, is to recognize that the current Iranian regime is in a de facto state of belligerency against the West, and to conduct the war from our side through political means, primarily by separating the Iranian people from the Iranian regime. Timmerman's and Woolsey's specific suggestions for conducting such a war—including extensive public diplomacy, massive financing of reform groups in Iran, economic sanctions to defund the regime's adventurism, and revamped western broadcasting to Iran—may be found in their works referenced in the notes at the end of this book. The primary point to be stressed here is that, if deterrence cannot work vis-à-vis Iran, something must be made to work. And if the strategic goal in Iran is regime change, which both the magnitude of the threat and the likely impossibility of deterrence suggest it must be, then specific tactics must be aimed at effecting regime change in Tehran as soon as possible. Whatever the passions of the apocalyptics in control of the Iranian government, it is not easy to believe that the majority of the Iranian people are eager to become a national suicide bomb. That suggests a direction for policy even at this late date.

A policy of regime change in Iran will not be easy to sell in a world accustomed to appeasement. That is why a declared policy of regime change in Iran ought to be accompanied by a bold and dramatic stroke on the part of the United States, suggested in early 2007 by former secretaries of state George P. Shultz and Henry A. Kissinger, former secretary of defense William J. Perry, and former senator Sam Nunn: the United States should, in concert with as many allies as it can gather, particularly from among the present nuclear powers, declare that its settled policy is the pursuit, over time and with careful monitoring, of the abolition of nuclear weapons throughout the world. Shultz and his colleagues fear, with good reason, that "the world is now on the precipice of a new and dangerous nuclear era" in which "non-state terrorists" are "conceptually outside the boundaries of a deterrent strategy." Moreover, and with reference to new nuclear-weapons states, Shultz and his colleagues warn that "it is far from certain that we can successfully replicate the old Soviet-American" patterns of deterrence through mutual assured destruction "with an increasing number of potential nuclear enemies worldwide without dramatically increasing the risk that nuclear weapons will be used." Why? Because "new nuclear states do not have the benefit of years of step-by-step safeguards put into effect during the Cold War to prevent nuclear accidents, misjudgments, or unauthorized launches." Nor, these senior statesmen might have added, was Soviet utopianism the same sort of thing as Iranian Shiite apocalypticism.

Thus Shultz and his colleagues strongly urge the United States, in concert with other present nuclear powers, to revive "the goal of an agreement to get rid of all nuclear weapons," as explored by Ronald Reagan and Mikhail Gorbachev at the Reykjavik summit in 1987. Shultz and his colleagues are under no delusions about the difficulty of the task they propose, but they also outline specific steps that would get the process started and demonstrate the seriousness of intent of the present nuclear powers.[10] Most important, they believe, is setting the goal, for, as they write, "without the bold vision, the actions [proposed] will not be perceived as fair or urgent." Energetic efforts to promote regime change in Iran or to deny Iran nuclear weapons can be perceived (and in fact have been spun by Iranian propaganda) as an effort to keep the new kid on the block out of the club. Energetic efforts at regime change in Tehran coupled with a U.S.-led campaign to give effect to the ultimate goal of nuclear weapons abolition—a goal contained in the very Nuclear Non-Proliferation Treaty to which we are trying to hold countries like Iran accountable—could help change the dynamics of this volatile situation, and in a good direction.

In his bestseller *Letter to a Christian Nation*, one of the most vocal of the new atheists, Sam Harris, declares that, as the world cannot survive both passionately held religious belief and weapons of mass destruction, passionately held religious belief must go. That thoroughly unrealistic prescription is likely to have as little effect in Tehran as it will in Nebraska. Yet, again, deterrence really is not an option any longer. While seeking regime change in states that simply cannot be permitted to possess nuclear weapons, the far wiser and more realistic course is that proposed by Messrs. Shultz, Perry, Kissinger, and Nunn: not to eliminate religious conviction, but to eliminate nuclear weapons.

Finally, before leaving the subject of deterrence, a word about the ongoing drama of Iraq.

Any deterrence value—in the very limited sense of a dampening of jihadist enthusiasms—that might have been expected to have been gained from the liberation of Iraq will be lost if the outcome there is widely believed to be an American defeat. Such an outcome would be a strategic, political, and moral catastrophe. It will be a catastrophe for the long-suffering Iraqis. It will be a catastrophe for U.S. and western security, because an imploding Iraq will become, like pre-9/11 Afghanistan, a safe haven for al-Qaeda and similar organizations. And it will be a catastrophe because of the signal of weakness it will send throughout the jihadist world, which under-

stands what so many antiwar activists and politicians seemingly cannot–that Iraq is now the strategic
center of gravity in the war against jihadist terrorism.

It may be that the final outcome in Iraq is not, ultimately, of our determining: that the future of Iraq
will inevitably come down to the question of
whether Iraqis want a state–even a loosely federal
state–more than they want to kill each other. But of
one thing we can be sure: the premature abandon-
ment of the effort to prevent that nightmare scenario
from playing itself out would be read by global jihadists as a sign of fecklessness that will have un-
told, but surely awful, consequences.

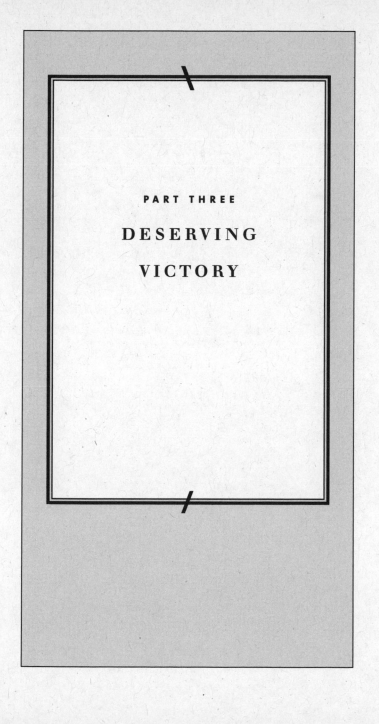

PART THREE

DESERVING
VICTORY

LESSON 11. Cultural self-confidence is indispensable to victory in the long-term struggle against jihadism.

London's Cabinet War Rooms, underneath Whitehall, are a splendid museum—and a reminder of the consequences that can follow when the political imagination of the democracies fails in the face of an existential threat. The Cabinet War Rooms are a monument to the leadership of Winston Churchill during the darkest days of World War II; but a visit there should also remind us of Churchill's wry suggestion that that struggle should have been dubbed "The Unnecessary War," as it could have been prevented by political wit and nerve in the 1930s. There is nothing "unnecessary" about the war against jihadism that has been declared upon us. Still, that Churchillian summons to political imagination and cultural nerve remains as salient as ever.

So does another Churchillian admonition from that period. The last time I visited the Cabinet War Rooms, I picked up a postcard copy of a British World War II poster, in which Churchill, looking very much the bulldog, points a stubby finger at you over the emblazoned slogan "Deserve Victory!" In democracies, in which the virtues of the citizenry are the foundations of national security, that is a motto for all seasons. It is a particularly apt one now.

What must we do to remedy our own incapacities, in order to deserve victory in the war against global jihadism? The first step is to recognize our most basic problems for what they are: problems in the order of ideas and of culture.

Marcello Pera is a former president of the Italian Senate, a philosopher of science in the line of Karl Popper, an agnostic—and a man with a penetrating analysis of the current crisis of civilizational morale that besets Europe. That crisis is not limited to Europe, however; elements of it can easily be found in the United States. Thus, what Senator Pera has to say about Europe's incapacities in the face of jihadism should be taken to heart by Americans, too: "Europe is infected by an epidemic of relativism. It believes that all cultures are equivalent. It refuses to judge them, thinking that to accept and defend one's own culture would be an act of hegemony, of intolerance, that betrayed an anti-democratic, anti-liberal, disrespectful attitude toward the autonomy of other populations and individuals."[1]

These indicators suggest a culture far more given to self-deprecation than to critical self-affirmation. A culture addicted to self-deprecation is unlikely to be able to defend its commitments to, say, democracy and the rule of law. A culture in which the habit, the

virtue, of self-critique and self-correction has deteri-
orated into self-contempt is a culture that is unlikely
to be able to meet the challenge of a self-confident
culture in the war of ideas—including moral ideas. A
relatively coherent culture—a culture that we believe
worth preserving, not simply a culture we accept
because it validates our private interests—is a prerequisite for winning the war against global jihadism. We will neither deserve victory nor achieve
it if we do not deem ourselves and our culture wor-
thy of victory.

A culture addicted to self-deprecation is the kind
of culture that produces what Christopher Hitchens
has called "one-way multiculturalism," which is not
pluralism rightly understood but rather the domestic version of what political analyst David Kelly has
styled the "preemptive cringe." Genuine pluralism—
Richard John Neuhaus's "engagement of differences
within the bond of civility"—requires mature self-
confidence; genuine pluralism cannot be built on a
foundation of self-contempt.[2]

The second half of Pope Benedict XVI's September
2006 Regensburg Lecture (which in fact occupied
far more than half of his text) was a sober reminder
to the West that, if irrational faith poses one grave
threat to the human future, so, too, does a loss of
faith in reason. For if the West loses its faith in the
human capacity to know the truth of anything with
certainty, it will have disarmed itself intellectually,
culturally, and morally, unable to give an account of

its commitments to civility, tolerance, the free society, and democratic self-government. Or, as Daniel Henninger nicely puts it, saying no to moral insouciance is very much part of "homeland security."[3] To which might be added the imperative of a "no" to the spiritual boredom and skepticism about our ability to know anything with certainty that inform moral insouciance.

The recovery of a mature cultural confidence in the West requires that we be able to defend western commitments to civil society and democracy philosophically; it also requires us to be able to defend those commitments historically. That is, we must reclaim the history of the West, including its modern democratic politics, as an outgrowth of the distinctive culture that was formed from the fruitful interaction of Jerusalem, Athens, and Rome: biblical religion, philosophical rationality, and law. The Whig theory of history—which tells the story of the West as if the freedom project in contemporary western public life only began with the Enlightenment—is mistaken, as a matter of the history of ideas. It also plays into the hands of jihadist ideologues, who are all too eager to claim that democracy, civil society, and the rule of law as we understand those terms are the by-products of decadent, godless cultures. In the war of ideas that is a crucial front in the war against jihadism, that slander must be met—not only because it falsifies the historical record, but because tracing the religious roots of the contemporary West's com-

mitments to civility in society and the method of persuasion in politics builds a bridge of genuine dialogue to those Muslims who wish to resist jihadism,
and who want for themselves political communities
that respect the dignity of the human person—political communities in which government is both responsible and responsive.

What did Christianity, to take a case in point, contribute to the evolution of the freedom project in the
West? Christianity taught that, while Caesar was to
be given his due, so was God (see Matthew 22:21).
And if there are things of God that are not Caesar's,
then Caesar's power is, by definition, limited power.
Augustus Caesar, John Courtney Murray reminds
us, "was both *Summus Imperator* and *Pontifex Max-
imus*; the *ius divinum* [divine law] was simply a part
of the *ius civile* [civil law]." Or, to put it a bit more
simply, Augustus combined in himself both the fullness of political/legal authority and the fullness of
spiritual authority, such that the things of God were
simply a department of the political community.
"The new Christian view," Murray argues, "was
based on a radical distinction between the order of
the sacred and the order of the secular." This was
revolutionary. The empire, which would later evolve
into what we know as the "state," was forced to share
"space" with another actor claiming real authority in
important areas of life—the Church.[4]

The Christian Church proclaimed a human dignity that was inalienable: a dignity that was neither

the by-product of social status or wealth, nor a boon conferred by the state. That proclamation, in turn, dramatically changed the relationship of the individual to the political community. It also changed our ideas of what the political community is and what its boundaries are. As what we now know as the "state" evolved in a West that had broken from the emperor/high priest monopoly of power in the pre-Christian world, the state was not the sum total of "society." The state was one set of functions within society, and the state came to be understood as the servant of society, not the other way around. By stripping political authority of the mantle of the sacred, Christianity helped create the possibility of what we know as "limited government": government that has specific and enumerated powers, government that ought not reach into that sphere of conscience where, as Pope John Paul II used to put it, men and women are in conversation with God. The first of human rights in the West—religious freedom—is not, in a long view of history, a pragmatic accommodation; it is the statement of a fundamental truth about the human person that has profound implications for the limited state.

The Christian-influenced concept of the rights-bearing individual as a member of a society that assigns certain limited functions to the state also implied a morally driven view of politics: politics is part of the moral universe, the universe of right and wrong, not simply an arena in which interests clash.

There are truths built into the world and into us; we can know them by an exercise of reason—and thus the laws we make should reflect "the dictates of reason, not sheer will."[5] The individual as bearer of rights in a limited state is also an individual in free association with others. Therefore, the state must respect the independence of families and of all those voluntary associations that human beings create to pursue legitimate economic, cultural, social, and religious purposes. The rich social pluralism of the West did not just happen. It emerged in a society formed by the biblical idea of the dignity óf the human person and the culture that epic idea shaped.[6]

The political thought that emerged from the Enlightenment had a profound effect in creating the political institutions of freedom in the West. That thinking emerged from, and those institutions were subsequently built on, cultural foundations set much more deeply—foundations set long before the Enlightenment, in the history of a West profoundly shaped by a lakeside conversation about whether a disciple of Jesus of Nazareth ought to pay taxes to Caesar.

Then there is the intellectual curiosity that is a distinctive hallmark of western civilization. It, too, was shaped by religious conviction: in this case, the conviction (reiterated by Benedict XVI at Regensburg) that God created the world through his "Word," through the divine reason—a theological idea that implies that the world can be understood by the arts of intelligence. It was not a fortuitous accident that the scientific method was developed in a culture that had long affirmed the intelligibility of the world, and had made that affirmation for the weightiest of reasons: the "reason" of God built things that way. This biblical conviction has, of course, been a tremendous material asset to the West, in terms of the technological accomplishments to which it ultimately gave birth. It is also the root of that unique western phenomenon, curiosity about other cultures and civilizations, which, as Bernard Lewis reminds us, led "to the discovery and decipherment of the monuments of the ancient Middle East, and the restoration, to the peoples of that region, of the great, glorious, and long forgotten past," which had been largely ignored by the region's Muslim rulers.[7]

A little more than a year after 9/11, French prime minister Jean-Pierre Rafferin referred in the French National Assembly to Saladin as the man who had been able to "liberate Jerusalem" from . . . well, from Prime Minister Rafferin's ancestors, the French Crusaders. One learned historian described Rafferin's choice of verb as "a rather extreme case of realignment of loyalties." Less politely, this is bizarre. It is also very dangerous.[8]

A West that sees in its past nothing but pathology—racism, colonialism, religious wars and persecutions, sexism, and all the rest—is a West that cannot, and almost certainly will not, defend its present. A West that can't remember its past accurately will not be able to project itself imaginatively into the future. A West that has airbrushed from its collective memory the contributions of biblical religion to its present freedoms is a West that is in a poor position to meet the challenge of a religiously shaped alternative reading of the past, present, and future. As British philosopher Roger Scruton writes, the West must be able and willing to demonstrate to the rest of the world, and to Muslims who believe that "western success and prosperity [are] . . . the products of a purely secular, even atheistic creed," that the greatest achievements of the West are not material but are, rather, "works of spiritual grace and high culture that transmit eternal meanings."[9]

Saying no to moral insouciance, then, means saying no as well to historical amnesia, and no to a crudely secular reading of the roots of the freedom project that is now under assault, and that we must defend.

LESSON 12. Islamist salami tactics must be resisted, for small concessions in the name of a false idea of tolerance inevitably lead to further concessions, and then to further erosions of liberty and security.

The terrorist threat that global jihadism poses to western societies is, or ought to be, difficult to miss: it is kinetic and obvious, even if its deepest sources are poorly understood. The radicalizing effects of jihadist theology and ideology on other Islamists, however, pose another serious, if more subtle, threat to the future of the West. For western societies may succumb to various cultural, social, and political pressures from Islamists and, in the name of a mistaken idea of tolerance, indulge themselves in forms of multiculturalism that lead, over time, to self-imposed dhimmitude—the reduction of non-Muslim populations to de facto second-class status in their own countries, by their own acquiescence to Islamist pressures.

This process is ominously well advanced in parts

of western Europe today. History, like nature, dis-
likes vacuums, and the demographic vacuum
caused by several generations of self-destructive
birthrates in Europe has been filled by a large-scale
immigration from throughout the Islamic world.
The most obvious effect of that immigration is on
display in continental Europe's increasingly segregated urban landscape, in which an impoverished
Muslim suburban periphery surrounds an affluent
European urban core; in Great Britain, by contrast,
large Muslim inner-city areas throughout the country seem to exist in a different civilizational orbit
than the rest of the country. Far more has changed in
Europe than the physical appearances of the continent's metropolitan areas, however.

There are, for example, dozens of "ungovern-
able areas" in France: Muslim-dominated suburbs,
mainly, where the writ of French law does not run
and the French police do not go. Similar extraterri-
torial enclaves, in which shari'a law is enforced by
local Muslim clerics, can be found elsewhere in
Europe, including the United Kingdom. While there
are some signs of political restlessness with these
arrangements, European public authorities have,
in the main, paid little or no attention these past
decades to practices among their Muslim populations that range from the physically cruel (female
circumcision) through the morally cruel (forced
marriages) to the socially disruptive (remanding
Muslim children back to radical madrassas in the

Middle East, North Africa, and Pakistan for their primary and secondary educations) and the illegal ("honor" killings in cases of adultery and rape—the female rape victim being the one killed).

European governments have not just looked the other way at these practices, however. European welfare systems generously support immigrants who sometimes despise their host countries and, in some cases, turn violently against them—most dramatically (and lethally) in the London Underground and bus bombings of July 7, 2005. As British columnist Melanie Phillips wrote, these London bombers were

> British boys, the product of British schools and universities and the British welfare system, [who] behaved in a way that repudiated not just British values but the elementary codes of humanity. Nor were they oddball loners. What caused them to go into the Tube with their backpacks and blow themselves and their fellow Britons to bits was an ideology that had taken hold like a cancer, not just in the madrassas of Pakistan but in the streets of Leeds and Bradford, Oldham and Leicester, Glasgow and Luton.[1]

But perhaps this is not so surprising in a country in which not a single Muslim cleric condemned as an offense against Islam the fatwa pronounced by Ayatollah Khomeini against the novelist Salman

Rushdie—a country in which prisons, heavily pop-
ulated by Muslims, are recruiting grounds for
jihadism because the prison authorities allow
seditious clerics and seditious materials to circulate
freely among their charges. These practices, bad
enough in themselves, have also led to the denial of
reality that Daniel Johnson has described as moral
inversion: "rather than accepting responsibility for
the jihadists in their midst, British Muslims have demanded that the government redress their own
grievances, whether about Israel and Iraq or about
the status in Britain of shari'a law. As [Sir Iqbal]
Sacranie [secretary-general of the Muslim Council
of Great Britain] declared after the attacks on London, 'the real victim of these attacks is the Muslim
community in the U.K.' " [2] What some of those jihadists
have in mind was made clear when BBC's Channel
4 surreptitiously taped a sermon by Dr. Ijaz Mian at
the Ahl-el-Hadith mosque in Derby:

> King, Queen, House of Commons: if you accept
> it, you are a part of it. If you don't accept it, you
> have to dismantle it. So you being a Muslim,
> you have to fix a target. There will be no House
> of Commons. From that White House to this
> Black House, we know we have to dismantle
> it. Muslims must grow in strength, then take
> over. . . . You are in a situation in which you
> have to live like a state-within-a-state—until
> you take over. [3]

It gets worse, however. Seditious Muslim crimi-
nals are often treated in Europe in ways that seem
dangerously reminiscent of Lewis Carroll's Red
Queen, with her world of impossible things before
breakfast. Thus Muhammad Bouyeri, the Dutch-
Moroccan who murdered filmmaker Theo van Gogh
in 2004 in the middle of an Amsterdam street and af-
fixed a personal fatwa to his victim's chest with a
kitchen knife, retains the right to vote—and could, if
he wished, run for the Dutch parliament. Mean-
while, at least two Dutch parliamentarians critical of
Islamist extremism were forced by Islamist threats
to live in prison or army compounds under police or
military guard.

These legal and political examples of self-imposed
dhimmitude had their origins in salami-cut concessions that escalated over the years. Thus French public swimming pools were segregated by sex because
of Muslim protests. "Piglet" mugs disappeared from
certain British retailers after Muslim complaints that
the *Winnie the Pooh* character offended Muslim
sensibilities. So, too, did Burger King chocolate ice-
cream swirls, which reminded some Muslims of Arabic script from the Qur'an. Several years ago, the
British Red Cross banned Christmas trees and nativ-
ity scenes from its charity stores for fear of offending
Muslims; for similar reasons, Dutch police destroyed
a piece of Rotterdam street art that read "Thou Shalt
Not Kill" in the wake of the van Gogh murder.
Schoolchildren in the Netherlands were forbidden to

display Dutch flags on their backpacks because immigrants might think them a provocation; again, for similar reasons–avoiding a "provocation"–a man in a restaurant beneath the Norwegian parliament was asked in 2006 to remove his jacket, on which he wore a Star of David, because this display was deemed a "provocation."

The 2006 Danish cartoons controversy–or, better, the Danish cartoons jihad–brought these patterns of appeasement and self-imposed dhimmitude to international attention. Despite the fact that the Danish government of the time was beginning to address some of the problems of Islamic nonintegration into Danish society, the original publication in the Copenhagen daily *Jyllands-Posten* of a set of cartoons depicting the Prophet Muhammad caused little comment, in Denmark or anywhere else. But after several Islamist Danish imams began agitating throughout the Middle East (aided by three additional, and far more offensive, cartoons of their own devising), an international furor erupted, with dozens of people killed by rioting Muslims in Europe, Africa, and Asia. As Henrik Bering wrote at the time, "the Danes were suddenly the most hated people on earth, with their embassies under attack, their flag being burned, and their consciousness being raised by lectures on religious tolerance from Iran, Saudi Arabia, and other beacons of enlightenment."

And the response from Europe, in the main, was to intensify appeasement.

Thus the French government encouraged the French Union of Islamic Organizations and the Grand Mosque of Paris to sue the satirical weekly *Charlie Hebdo* in order to prevent the magazine's publication of the cartoons; when the suit was thrown out, French president Jacques Chirac offered Muslim groups the services of his personal lawyer in order to help them file suit against the magazine's editor on charges of racism.[4] The Italian "reforms minister," Roberto Calderoli, resigned under pressure from Prime Minister Silvio Berlusconi, because Calderoli had worn a T-shirt featuring one of the offending cartoons–which "thoughtless action," Berlusconi deduced, had caused a riot outside the Italian consulate in Benghazi in which eleven people were killed. Newspapers that ran the cartoons were put under intense political pressure; some journalists faced criminal charges; websites were forced to close. The pan-European Carrefour supermarket chain, bowing to Islamist demands for a boycott of Danish goods, placed signs in its stores, in both Arabic and English, expressing "solidarity" with the "Islamic community" and noting, inelegantly if revealingly, "Carrefour don't carry Danish products." The Norwegian government forced the editor of a Christian publication to apologize publicly for printing the Danish cartoons, at a press conference at which the hapless editor was surrounded (appropriately enough) by Norwegian cabinet ministers and imams. EU foreign minister Javier Solana groveled his way from one Arab capital to another, pleading that Europeans shared the "anguish" of Muslims "offended" by the Danish cartoons. And, not to be outdone by those appeasement-obsessed national governments that were in headlong flight from traditional concepts of freedom of the press and free speech, the EU's justice minister, Franco Frattini, announced in early February 2006 that the EU would establish a "media code" to encourage "prudence." Which in this instance was a synonym for "surrender"–irrespective of one's view of the artistic merits of, or the cultural sensitivity displayed by, the world's most notorious cartoons.

Becoming a *dhimmi* is not always a matter of accommodating to the strictures of an imposed Islamic law. As the European experience demonstrates, self-imposed dhimmitude is a danger when the nature of tolerance is misunderstood as the avoidance of differences. When democratic states with a record of genuine tolerance that puts most Islamic societies to shame turn themselves inside out legally in order to appease seditious extremists, they betray their own constituting principles and lay the cultural groundwork for further trouble in the future.

Americans should not imagine that such self-imposed dhimmitude is impossible here. To take but one example: like their European counterparts, American prisons are a fertile ground for recruitment to jihadism, thanks to the widespread distribution of Wahhabi materials and the prominence of

Wahhabi clerics as prison chaplains. Given an understanding of what is at stake, however, the political will to demand change, and the wit to fight the inevitable legal battles that will ensue, such problems may be more easy to fix than the attitude of preemptive appeasement that can work its way through a culture. It was, at the very least, instructive that the National Football League rejected a 2007 Super Bowl ad for the U.S. Border Patrol because the proposed ad mentioned fighting terrorism. "The ad that the department submitted was specific to [the] Border Patrol and it mentioned terrorism. We were not comfortable with that," said NFL spokesman Greg Aiello.[5] Immediately after 9/11, you may recall, the NFL ordered that small American flags be displayed on all its players' helmets. A nice patriotic gesture, that, but a hollow one when the NFL forgets just what it is that the flag represents and kowtows to some who might take exception at the mere mention of a terrorist threat being posed by people attempting to enter the country illegally.

More than resistance to Islamist salami tactics is required, however. In the war of ideas that is an essential front in the war against jihadism, the West in general, and the United States in particular, must go on the offensive. This means making the promotion of religious freedom a priority in the interreligious dialogue, and a priority in the foreign policy of the United States and other western governments.

Neither governments, nor public officials, nor

diplomats can do what Pope Benedict XVI did in his September 2006 Regensburg Lecture: authoritatively identify, analyze, and critique the theological roots of jihadism as they are found in defective understandings of the nature of God. What governments, elected public officials, and the diplomats representing the United States and other western democracies can do, and indeed must do, is deal more forthrightly with the bad public effects of bad theology. I vividly recall a meeting in the Roosevelt Room of the White House's West Wing shortly after the end of the first Gulf War. President George H. W. Bush was slightly late for a meeting with religious leaders and religious intellectuals who had been supportive of his administration's policy, so a senior National Security Council official was brought in to take our questions. I noted that the United States had just saved the Kingdom of Saudi Arabia from the dubious pleasure of becoming the twentieth province of Greater Iraq; what, I asked the NSC official, did we now propose to do about the state of religious freedom in Saudi Arabia, where public celebrations of Christian worship were forbidden and tourist Bibles routinely confiscated and destroyed? The official turned the color of dough, cleared his throat, and said that he didn't think raising such issues with the Saudis was a very wise idea.

That, again, is self-imposed dhimmitude—although it reflects an attitude that is widely shared in the U.S. foreign policy establishment (of which the aforementioned official is an epigone) and in the elite universities that form the intellectual core of that establishment. Given appropriate direction from the administration they serve, America's professional diplomats will take up specific cases of religious persecution. But the steady, purposeful, long-term promotion of religious freedom—or, at the very least, religious toleration—seems beyond the imagining of much of the State Department (not to mention the Council on Foreign Relations). Yet how can responsible and responsive governments evolve in the Islamic world if the first of human rights is regularly and systematically denied? The unspoken consensus in the secularist world of the American foreign policy establishment seems to be that responsible and responsive government in the Islamic world will only follow some form of secularization—but that is to make the same mistake that neo-atheist Sam Harris makes on the question of religious conviction and weapons of mass destruction. Religious conviction is *not* going away. Surely the point, for governments as well as for Christian interreligious dialogue partners, is to support the work of those Muslims who are trying to develop an Islamic case for religious tolerance within societies characterized by a genuine pluralism of differences engaged with respect. No one need expect that that will be an easy task, or one swiftly accomplished. But if American foreign policy analysts and diplomats continue to miss a crucial fact of international public life—that religious conviction plays as important a role in shaping world politics as the political and economic indicators they're trained to recognize and assess—our diplomatic reading of the signs of the times will suffer commensurately.

Religious freedom is not a private matter, nor is contending for religious freedom a kind of optional humanitarianism. It is a matter of self-respect, in that we believe—or ought to believe—that our own commitment to religious freedom reflects a universal moral truth written on the human heart, such that a core principle of our culture is at stake here, for believers and nonbelievers alike. It is also a matter of making the world safe for diversity by helping Islamic countries develop the capacity for diversity within themselves. Anyone who doubts that that is an urgent issue—and perhaps *the* most urgent issue—for the twenty-first century should think back to that cave in Tora Bora and recall precisely what it was that put Osama bin Laden there.

LESSON 13. We cannot, and will not, deserve victory (much less achieve it) if we continue to finance those who attack us. Therefore, a program to defund jihadism by developing alternatives to petroleum-based transportation fuels is a crucial component of the current struggle.

Global jihadism would not be the threat it is had the West not transferred some $2 trillion in wealth to the Arab Islamic world since World War II–which, among other things, has allowed Saudi Arabia to spend an estimated $70–$100 billion spreading Wahhabi doctrine and its summons to jihadist sedition and violence all over the globe.[1] Irrespective of one's conclusions about the magnitude of the threat that fossil fuel emissions pose to the environment, the national security threat of oil dependency is obvious. It is also self-demeaning, a habit that must be broken–and can be, given the proper application of technological imagination and political will.

Then there is the global dimension. The world's reliance on oil from the Middle East and Iran, where two-thirds of proven global conventional oil reserves are located, has now distorted world politics for three generations. That, too, is a very good reason to move as smartly as possible—and in both senses of "smartly"—toward a different kind of world: not one in which oil plays no role (for that is impossible), but a world in which oil is a far less prominent protagonist in global politics and economics.

This is not the place to address all the issues involved in a national energy policy aimed at a far greater measure of energy independence, nor would I be competent to do so. If the focus here is on defunding jihadism by dramatically reducing the flow of oil revenues to the Middle East and Persian Gulf, however, there ought to be broad agreement on R. James Woolsey's argument that "energy independence for the U.S. is . . . preponderantly a problem related to oil and its dominant role in fueling vehicles for transportation."[2] In March 2006 testimony before the Senate Energy Committee, Woolsey outlined several reasons why reliance on petroleum products for the bulk of the world's transportation energy is intolerably dangerous. The petroleum infrastructure, here and abroad, is vulnerable to terrorist attack; a well-coordinated terrorist attack that took down the sulphur-clearing towers at the Abqaiq refinery complex in Saudi Arabia could cost the world market five to six million barrels of oil *per day*. Should Islamist or jihadist-dependent governments come into power in certain Middle Eastern countries, they could institute embargoes or other supply disruptions that would cause severe economic dislocations, in the United States and globally. And, as noted above, wealth transfers due to oil imports fund jihadist terrorism and its ideological support structure. We are, in a word, dangerously vulnerable, politically, economically, and existentially, because of the magnitude of our oil dependence for our transportation needs. And this must stop.[3]

Woolsey then proposed two strategic directions through which U.S. government policy could address this vulnerability using either existing technologies or technologies that can be brought into the market quickly and that can work within today's transportation infrastructure. Government policy should, in Woolsey's view, "(1) encourage a shift to substantially more fuel-efficient vehicles . . . including promoting both battery development and a market for existing battery types for plug-in hybrid vehicles; and (2) encourage biofuels and other alternative and renewable fuels that can be produced from inexpensive and widely available feedstocks–wherever possible from waste products."[4]

Writing in the *Wall Street Journal* at the end of 2006, Woolsey, like others, stressed that while supposed silver bullets–such as the corn-based ethanol that briefly seized the imagination of the media and the Congress–aren't the answer, there are, nonetheless, steps responsible government can take to encourage a market-driven shift toward a portfolio of alternative fuels for transportation, steps that could put a significant dent in American oil imports over the next several decades:

> Subsidizing expensive substitutes for petroleum, ignoring the massive infrastructure costs needed to fuel family cars with hydrogen, searching for a single elegant solution—none of this has worked, nor will it. Instead, we should encourage a portfolio of inexpensive fuels, including electricity, that requires very little infrastructure change and let its components work together. A 50 m.p.g. hybrid, once it becomes a plug-in, will likely get solidly over 100 m.p.g. of gasoline (call it 'm.p.g.g.'); if it is also a flexible fuel vehicle using 85% ethanol, E-85, its m.p.g.g. rises to around 500. The market will likely operate to expand sharply the use of these technologies that are already in pilot plants and prototypes and heavily reduce oil use in the foreseeable future.[5]

David Sandalow, an energy and environment scholar at the Brookings Institution, takes a similar approach, proposing a broad-based strategy that would result in "transformational change" in the fuel structure of the American transportation system. Agreeing with Woolsey on the portfolio approach, Sandalow argues for a mix of private-sector initiatives and governmental policies, the net effect of which would be to give drivers realistic and afford-able choices between petroleum-based products and other fuels. Plug-in hybrids, biofuels (like cellulosic ethanol), and the use of high-strength/low-weight composites in automobile manufacture could, work-ing together, end America's overwhelming depen-dence on oil as transportation fuel "in a generation," he (perhaps boldly) concludes.[6]

Federal policy, Sandalow argues, has a catalytic role here: it should aim deliberately at transforming the present national auto fleet through massive fed-eral purchases of plug-in hybrids (when these be-come available); through a "grand bargain" with Detroit, in which a federal trust fund is established to absorb the costs of retired auto workers' health care, which drain funds needed for research and de-velopment, "in exchange for [the industry's] invest-ments in fuel-saving technologies"; and through substantial tax credits to purchasers of fuel-efficient automobiles, funded by the twenty-cent-per-gallon tax on gasoline that 55 percent of Americans tell pollsters they would support if such a tax increase reduced American dependence on foreign oil. A corollary benefit of such a transformational effort, Sandalow concludes, would be the revitalization of the now-sclerotic American automobile industry.[7]

Like Woolsey's, Sandalow's recommendations are both/and, rather than either/or—America needs both new fuels and increased fuel efficiency in its transportation vehicles; American needs both biofuels (including, but certainly not limited to, cellulosic ethanol) and plug-in hybrids–so that, over a generation, a portfolio of solutions work together to reduce transportation-related oil dependence dramatically, and thus dramatically defund jihadism. To those who object that Middle Eastern oil producers will simply find other markets for oil–such as China–Woolsey and Sandalow reply that China has no desire to become dependent on the volatile Middle East for energy supplies, and that a new "oil diplomacy," aimed not only at weaning America away from oil dependency but at helping other economies do the same, is the answer. As Sandalow writes, "Fuel efficiency improvements in China could do more to protect our national security, fight global warming, and promote economic growth than additional supply from the Persian Gulf."[8] As for the reaction of Saudi Arabia to the declaration of the kind of American energy strategy suggested here, there would undoubtedly be some short-term difficulties. But the argument can be made that the less America, the West, and the rest of the world need Saudi Arabia, the better Saudi Arabia will behave.

While there are no magic solutions to oil dependency, there are specific, realistic steps that can and should be taken toward that end. The United States can, by the exercise of its national imagination and will, and with leadership from both the public and private sectors, defund global jihadism by drastically cutting the transfer of funds related to petroleum imports for transportation use—en route to a more rational national energy policy. It beggars belief that peoples who did not discover a resource, much less the means to exploit it and make it the source of vast wealth, have profited by its development in ways that now threaten the very possibility of world order. This is self-imposed dhimmitude, if of a global economic sort. Its hold on our destiny must be ended, as a matter of self-defense as well as of self-respect.

LESSON 14. Victory in the war against global jihadism requires a new domestic political coalition that is proof against the confusions caused by the Unhinged Left and the Unhinged Right.

If this is indeed a moment analogous to the late 1940s—a moment when, like Truman and Acheson and Marshall and Vandenberg, we are "present at the creation"—we would do well to adopt a lesson from that period and create, if possible, a new, supple, bipartisan domestic political coalition that understands the nature and magnitude of the threat of global jihadism and is broadly agreed on the measures necessary to combat it and defeat it. I say "if possible," because any such new configuration would have to stand firmly against the capacity to distort the debate shown by both the Unhinged Left and the Unhinged Right since 9/11.

In a brilliant article published in early 2007, Mary Eberstadt adopted a trope from Bob Woodward and described in great detail the "denial" displayed by both the Unhinged Left and the Unhinged Right in the face of the new things of the post-9/11 world.[1] Elements of the Unhinged Left misdiagnose the present danger to the republic and displace responsibility for it onto the bogies called "neocons," "theocons," and "theocrats." A prominent liberal political theorist warns darkly about "American Eichmanns." Still others on the Left ignore the demographic foundations of world politics and boast of the West's infertility, worrying more about the disappearance of arctic polar bears than the disappearance of children.[2] Scientists produce bogus data about civilian casualties in Iraq and see it reported as hard news. A professional association of archaeologists denounces the (wildly exaggerated) looting of the Iraq Museum in Baghdad as "the most severe blow to cultural heritage in modern history, comparable to the sack of Constantinople [and] the burning of the library at Alexandria."[3]

And just about everyone caught in this particular slough of political despond thinks of George W. Bush as a figure perhaps (but only perhaps) one notch below the Antichrist in malignity. As British commentator Gerard Baker writes, "When one group of Muslims explodes bombs underneath the school buses of another group of Muslims in Baghdad or cuts the heads off humanitarian workers in Anbar, blame George Bush. When Vladimir Putin, the president of Russia, denounces an imbalanced world and growls about the unpleasantness of democracy in eastern Europe, blame George Bush. When the Earth's atmosphere gets a little more clogged with the output of power plants in China, India, and else-where, blame George Bush." Baker is no apologist for the Bush administration, but all of this strikes him as nothing less than "a comfortable substitute for think-ing hard about global challenges, a kind of intellec-tual escapism." The hard truth of the matter, Baker concludes, is that "the challenge of radical Islamism was not invented by the Bush Administration," a stark truth with which George Bush's successor will quickly have to reckon, beginning on Inauguration Day in January 2009.[4]

Then there is the starboard side of the political spectrum, where questions of modernity and its dis-contents loom large.

The vulgarities and self-absorption of late moder-nity are indeed a grave cultural problem, and a country whose principal exports include pornogra-phy and films saturated in violence weakens both its own moral culture and its capacity to make the case for freedom abroad. All that can and should be con-ceded—and addressed. Yet these vulgarities, inter-secting with more traditional forms of xenophobia, seem to have conspired in parts of the conservative political world to create an Unhinged Right with a serious problem of enemy identification. This, Mary Eberstadt suggested, was particularly evident in the 2005–2007 immigration debate, as some on the Un-hinged Right described "illegal immigration" as "the existential crisis of our time," threatening "the end of the United States as a sovereign self-sufficient inde-

pendent republic." No doubt the United States has
a serious problem to wrestle with when its immigration law becomes a virtual dead letter. And no
doubt one measure of the cultural and civic self-
confidence discussed above will be the capacity of
the United States to manage both its borders and its
immigration policies in a rational way. But "the existential crisis of our time"? Please. How many of those
Mexican illegals have flown 767s into office towers?[5]

There is a serious question as to whether the kind
of Truman-Vandenberg coalition that was assembled
in the late 1940s can be replicated today, given the
dependence of the Democratic Party on the Unhinged Left for funding and the seeming willingness
of Republicans upset about deficits, "No Child Left
Behind," budget-busting prescription drug benefits
for seniors, and the administration's proposals for
immigration reform to throw George W. Bush over
the side—irrespective of what would happen, in real-
world consequences and public perception, to his
administration's accurate identification of the principal threat to both U.S. national security and a mini-
mum of world order. Skepticism about the ability of
today's generation of politicians to rise to the standard of disinterested bipartisanship set in the immediate post–World War II period has also, alas, been
intensified by the performance of the Congress in recent years.

Congress, historically, tends to be a very blunt instrument when it comes to foreign and defense pol-

icy. Congressional attempts to micromanage the Union Army drove Lincoln to distraction during the Civil War. Congressional recalcitrance (combined with Woodrow Wilson's self-righteous stubbornness) prevented U.S. entry into the League of Nations after World War I, thus rendering that early effort at world order dead on arrival. The Smoot-Hawley tariffs passed by Congress in 1930 deepened the Great Depression. A decade later, the House of Representatives came within one vote of dismantling the United States Army, four months before Pearl Harbor. Congress wrote Lyndon Johnson a blank check in the 1965 Gulf of Tonkin resolution; a generation later, Congress tried to micromanage nuclear arms negotiations.

This pattern of strategic myopia and ineptness is, in fact, institutional in its origins—and it is worsening. Once, it was House members who were tethered to short, two-year electoral leashes, and thus vulnerable to rapid changes in public opinion. Now, the many senators who imagine themselves potential presidents in our ever-shortening election cycles are similarly on a poll-driven hair trigger. Under these circumstances, it was hardly surprising, in early 2007, when a supplemental appropriation to fund the war against jihadism in Iraq was suddenly encrusted with pork, including $27 million to deal with ravages to the domestic spinach crop and $74 million to "ensure proper storage for peanuts."[6] Unsurprising, but depressing nonetheless—and an ominous indicator of the self-promoting pandering that we can ill afford in times like these, which require political courage.

These institutional problems are further compounded today by issues of competence and comprehension. It was not reassuring in January 2007 when the chairman-designate of the House Select Committee on Intelligence did not know the difference between Sunni and Shia, and the relationship of Sunni and Shia to Hamas and Hezbollah. Yet the House Speaker who had named the ill-prepared Congressman Silvestre Reyes chairman of the Intelligence Committee (at a time when U.S. intelligence agencies needed to be put under the most critical scrutiny) had herself argued that "if we leave Iraq, then the insurgents leave Iraq, [and] the terrorists will leave Iraq."[7] At about the same time, Rep. Lynn Woolsey (D-California) rhetorically stamped her foot and demanded an early deadline for U.S. withdrawal from Iraq, declaring, "This nightmare must end"–as if the jihadist surge in Iraq since late 2003 were simply a bad dream that could be wished away.[8]

If the American people are willing to countenance incompetence, naïveté, and seemingly willful incomprehension in their elected officials, that is their sovereign prerogative. But it is an exercise of the people's sovereignty that is dangerous in the extreme. Both Congress and the American people must think long term about the war against jihadism. Which is to say that both Congress and the American

people must develop and nurture the virtue of patience. The country will have a hard time being pa-
tient, however, if the Congress insists on being an all
too easily redirected weathervane in its approach to
jihadism, blown this way and that by the shifting
tides of opinion and the latest media hype.

Thus, and to repeat: a new, bipartisan Coalition of
Those Who Understand is essential to victory in the
long-term war against jihadism. Were such a coalition to be formed, it should take as one of its tasks a
rationalization of our homeland security policy–
which is essential in deserving, and achieving, victory. We have not yet–perhaps–reached the point
of Great Britain, where one of the country's most
wanted terrorists slipped through Heathrow airport
in early 2007 by wearing a burqa, while Scottish
grandmothers bent over to remove their shoes and
belts at X-ray machines. But we are close enough:
on a recent flight out of Baltimore-Washington International Airport, I watched in amazement as
Transportation Security Administration employees
required a U.S. Army officer, dressed in desert fa-
tigues and displaying a valid, up-to-date military
identification card, to take off his boots in order to be
screened. This is both an absurd waste of time and
money and an insult to a serving officer; but it and
other idiocies will continue, and may intensify, unless Americans decide that effective counterterror-
ism is more important than political correctness in
devising airport screening measures–a matter on

which the airport store clerk who told me in disgust that those TSA screening apparatchiks should have "thanked the captain for risking his life for our country" showed far more sense than either the Congress or the Department of Homeland Security.

Our current, one-size-fits-all screening practices are estimated to cost billions of dollars a year, in both homeland security budgets and lost time. The monies sucked into this quicksand pit are also funds not being used to harden vulnerable parts of the national infrastructure—electricity grids, seaports, railroad yards, other cargo transshipment nodes—against terrorist attack or terrorist infiltration. Some day—after the next attack?—today's current, wasteful airport screening procedures could be applied to other forms of transportation. So now is the time to rethink all of this, before the rituals of degradation that currently accompany the once-simple act of boarding an airplane seriously erode the American people's patience—and their willingness to conduct a generations-long struggle against terrorism. Risk profiling and the development of trusted traveler identification cards would be two important elements in rationalizing homeland security.[9]

Similar PC problems bedevil military preparedness. Special Operations forces are, and will continue to be, a crucial military component in the war against global jihadism. Yet the Pentagon is under steady pressure to revise the rigorous training procedures that produce the kind of Special Operations forces we need. Why? To achieve some mythical, yet politically correct, gender balance in Special Ops forces. This must stop, and its cessation ought to be supported by the broadest possible political coalition.[10]

The rationalization of policy in the war against jihadism has a legal dimension, too. Some now use the term "lawfare" to describe the ways in which al-Qaeda and similar terrorist organizations use "international law claims, usually factually or legally meritless, as a tool of war," in which "the goal is to gain a moral advantage ... in the court of world opinion, and potentially a legal advantage in national and international tribunals."[11] Were these "lawfare" exercises successful, David Rivkin and Lee Casey warn, "their effect ... would be to make it exceptionally difficult—if not impossible—for a law-abiding state to wage war in anything like the traditional manner, by bringing the full weight of the national armed forces to bear against an enemy, without prompting charges of war crimes and efforts to intimidate individual officials with prosecutions on ersatz 'war crimes.' "[12] "Lawfare" tactics by jihadists are bad enough (and underscore the importance of a consistent and persistent U.S. public diplomacy that explains the moral and legal rationales for our actions, over and over again). But our own courts can also make the war against jihadism more difficult than it already is by putting irrational obstacles in the way of detecting terrorism plots.

Thus, according to a 2006 ruling by federal district court judge Anna Diggs Taylor, the U.S. government can alert Scotland Yard and MI5 if the National Security Agency intercepts a phone call from Peshawar to London in which jihadists plot to unleash a dirty radiological bomb in Trafalgar Square; but any such NSA intercept of a call between Kandahar and Chicago in which terrorists plot to set off a similar bomb at 16th Street and Pennsylvania Avenue is unconstitutional and records of it must be erased.[15] This is, quite literally, insane. And it, too, must stop. Only a Coalition of Those Who Understand that is bipartisan in character is likely to apply the brakes. And only a president who understands the nature, danger, and likely duration of the jihadist threat will appoint the kind of federal judges who will avoid such idiocies in the future.

LESSON 15. There is no escape from U.S. leadership.

The challenge of global jihadism cannot be avoided. Global jihadism cannot be appeased. Post-9/11 "exhaustion" is not an option; neither is failure. The war that has been declared against us–and by "us" I mean the West, not simply the United States–must be engaged, and through a variety of instruments, many of them not military.

There is, for example, the weapon of public diplomacy, which contributed to victory in the the Cold War but has rarely been unsheathed with effect since 9/11. By "public diplomacy" I mean the full range of resources the United States can deploy to fight the war of ideas in which we are engaged with global jihadism. If ideas have consequences, as they manifestly do, then the fact that the United States has done a singularly inept job of explaining, defending, and promoting its post-9/11 policies abroad has been every bit as much a defeat in the war against jihadism as losing the First Battle of Fallujah.

Public diplomacy–the careful, steady, persuasive explanation of U.S. policy in the war against global jihadism and the reasoning behind it—ought to be a priority of America's diplomatic representatives abroad. Thus appointments of American ambassadors in key countries around the world should be made with that task in mind: potential ambassadors should be screened, not primarily on the basis of their contributions to a president's most recent campaign, but for their ability to engage the local media, the local universities and think tanks, and all the other places in the host society where opinion is shaped and disseminated. That has not been the practice since 9/11, unfortunately, and the results have been dismal: the field has been left to the politically correct biases of the world media, which has exercised inordinate influence in shaping the terrain of public debate in ways often unfavorable to a serious understanding of the war against global jihadism. Thus in some of the most pro-American countries on earth, support for U.S. policy has eroded steadily since 9/11. There is no need for this, and there ought to be no excuse for it, either.

In addition to a more thoughtful set of criteria for political appointments to major embassies, the training of Foreign Service officers must be developed and recast in light of the demands of the war against jihadism. The problems of the secularist mind-set that prevails in the U.S. foreign policy establishment have been noted above. Those secularist default positions could begin to be reset if the training of Foreign Service officers included—on the model of existing tracks for arms control and economics specialists—a track that emphasized the role of religion (considered institutionally) and religious conviction (considered personally and in terms of culture formation) in shaping democratic cultures and world politics.

Challenging the assumption in the American foreign policy establishment that the only answer to global jihadism is to convert 1.2 billion Muslims into good secular liberals is only one facet of the more comprehensive Foreign Service reform needed, however. Foreign Service officers need specialized training in combating the anti-Americanism that has become a staple feature of international public life in recent years, often as the result of a bizarre coalition of Islamists and postmodern leftists.[1] Every U.S. embassy in a country crucial to the war against jihadism should have a specialist assigned to combating these trends through the arts of public diplomacy—just as U.S. embassies during the Cold War fought the battle of ideas against communism in Europe and Asia through attachés who had cut their ideological teeth in the U.S. labor wars of the 1930s. The precise contemporary parallel to those diplomatic idea warriors likely does not exist, but surely the lessons from that period could be distilled and brought to bear in the training of specialized public diplomacy Foreign Service officers.[2] It would, of course, be helpful if such specializations were understood within the Foreign Service to be tickets to promotion, not career dead ends.

There are other institutional measures that should be considered in a concerted effort to make dramatic improvements in America's public diplomacy capabilities. Core elements of the old U.S. Information Agency ought to be brought out of mothballs at the State Department and made part of the Executive Office of the President. A new White House office of public diplomacy, working in close proximity to a president who understood the imperatives of public diplomacy, would not be subject to the instinct for conflict aversion that is institutionally ingrained at Foggy Bottom (as it is in every other foreign ministry in the developed world). And from that more bureaucratically secure White House position, it could help devise an effective counter to the problems caused by al-Jazeera and similar Arab-language media.

These problems should not be underestimated. Another classic conceit of faux "realism" is to suggest that all this hearts-and-minds business is ephemera. It isn't, as American academics invited to lecture at such relatively stable and friendly Arab countries like Oman report—there, al-Jazeera spin sets the default positions of public debate, not the feeble efforts of the United States through its Arabic-language Radio Sawa service and the new al-Hurra television network. But why should this be surprising when fifty minutes of each hour on Radio Sawa (intended to replace the Arabic service of the Voice of America, which was shut down in 2002) is filled with pop music of the Eminem, J.Lo, and Britney Spears variety, rather than with serious discussions, hard news, and editorials explaining U.S. policy?

The mindlessness here is truly staggering. Media magnate Norman Pattiz, a Clinton appointee to the Broadcasting Board of Governors (which has oversight responsibility for government-funded overseas radio and television broadcasting), once told the *New Yorker* that "it was MTV that bought down the Berlin Wall." So, as former Voice of America director Robert Reilly wrote in early 2007, the war of ideas has been "transformed . . . into the battle of the bands." The results, thus far, are nonexistent. As Reilly wrote in a column with the apt title, "Britney vs. The Terrorists":

> After years of the United States broadcasting Britney Spears to the Levant, the average radical mullah has not exactly succumbed to apoplexy or come to love democracy. A State Department inspector general's draft report on Radio Sawa (the final report was never issued) found that "it is difficult to ascertain Radio Sawa's impact in countering anti-American views and the biased state-run media of the Arab world." Or, as one expert panel assembled to assess its value concluded, "Radio

Sawa failed to present America to its audience"... The condescension implicit in this
nearly all-music format is not lost on the audience that we wish to influence the most—those
who think.[3]

The solution? As Robert Reilly writes, "We need
radio broadcasting in the 'war of ideas,' but it has to
deal in ideas to be effective. The 'MTV message' is
something that commercial broadcasting can do and
would do better than government-funded radio.
Government broadcasting is needed when the
United States must communicate a message to a key
audience that that audience otherwise would not
hear." Thus future administrations must take far
more seriously the questions of defining the ideas
essential to winning the war against global jihadism
and devising ways to deploy those ideas, as Reilly
writes, "by all available means to the places that
most need to hear them."[4]

A parallel strategy for countering jihadist propaganda on the Internet, which has become a powerful
Islamist and jihadist weapon, must also be devised.
Islamist Internet initiatives like the "Voice of the
Caliphate" Internet broadcasting channel are not
shy about declaring their purposes: to "benefit the jihad fighters and bring grief to the infidels and the
hypocrites." Programs include video clips of jihadist
terror operations from Iraq, Afghanistan, Chechnya,
and Turkistan, and broadcasts of Osama bin Laden's

speeches.[5] The United States Government has, it seems, little effective defense against this kind of thing, which is pandemic on an Internet in which it is not difficult to find detailed instructions from veteran jihadists for destroying a U.S. M1A1 Abrams tank. Getting such defenses in place, soon, should be a priority.

Yet again, offense is as important as effective defense. There are numerous benefits to be gained from taking public diplomacy seriously. Challenging the seeming indifference of the "Arab street" to the slaughter of Arabs and fellow Muslims by al-Qaeda and others is important. Perhaps far more important, over the long haul, would be demonstrating, by effective international broadcasting and netcasting, that debate, criticism of others, and self-criticism do not equal weakness—which an Arab Islamic culture historically short on self-criticism regularly assumes. Assertive public diplomacy, especially through broadcasting and the Internet, could also help shake the intellectual cobwebs from the Islamic world, by reminding Muslims of a different Muslim history that existed before the onset of Arab authoritarianism. As Bernard Lewis has put it, it is important to remind Muslims that "traditional Islamic governments devoted great importance to consultation ... to limited authority, to government under law; all these things were part of the traditional Islamic background."[6]

Governmental efforts at public diplomacy are not

all there is on this crucial front in the global war against jihadism. Again, the lessons of the Cold War need to be relearned—or, in too many instances, learned. Nongovernmental organizations like the Congress for Cultural Freedom and journals like *Encounter* played important roles in winning the war of ideas in the Cold War. Where are their counterparts today? Might the wiser elements in American philanthropy take the lead in creating parallel organizations and publications for the twenty-first century?

Whatever the post-9/11 incapacities identified above—and they are serious, and they must be addressed—the fact remains that there is no alternative to U.S. leadership in the war against global jihadism. As Michael Gerson has put it, "There must be someone in the world capable of drawing a line—someone who says, 'This much and no further.' At some point, those who decide on aggression must pay a price, or aggression will be universal."[7] That someone—at least as a court of last instance—can only be the United States.

The United States is, to be sure, a very different kind of imperial power: what one analyst has described as a hybrid combining the roles of trading partner, lifeguard, and sheriff.[8] However new the model, it seems likely that only the United States can summon the coalition capable of resisting, and then reversing, and then defeating the jihadist tide: not only because the United States has the resources for the job, but because the United States is, or ought to be, the repository of the ideas, drawn from both faith and reason, that must shape that struggle.

Yale scholar David Gelernter, himself the victim of a terrorist (the Unibomber), proposed a script for the 2007 State of the Union Message that is worth citing at some length, and even more worth pondering, on this question of the unavoidability of American responsibility in the war in which we find ourselves:

> Our enemies in this war seem varied but share one common doctrine ... *all agree on death.* They believe in and cultivate death; they are the party of death. And we are the party of life—and they hate us for that and hope to destroy us because of it. No war we have ever fought is more fundamental than this.
>
> Obviously we can't confer life; can't even protect and preserve it—not always. But we do our best. Life comes from God, and we hope to be its champions. We told the world so in 1776; *life,* liberty, and the pursuit of happiness are the things we stood for. Those words echoed John Winthrop's as he sailed to Boston in 1630. He wrote about the city on a hill he hoped this land would become. He was quoting the Bible, and finished with another biblical verse: "Choose life and live, you and your children!" On those words we set to work and built this great American community.

We claim no special credit for being the party of life. We invite every person and people in the world to join us. The less exclusive the party, the better. But as champions of life, we have awful responsibilities ... [for] our enemies believe in death and say so plainly. Almost thirty years ago, Shiite fanatics gathered in Tehran to scream hatred at this nation; they weren't content with "down with America," they screamed "*death* to America" and meant it. The secular tyrant Saddam Hussein tortured and slaughtered his enemies and their little children. His terrorist friends believe in the same doctrine, "murder thy enemy." The random killing of men, women, and children inspires their supporters to dance in the streets. Fanatic Muslim clerics preach murder in their holy places. And on 9/11, al-Qaeda accomplished what even Hitler never did: the mass murder of American civilians.

These proud champions of death kill innocent people all over the world, and their own people at home; they have even discovered new ways to kill themselves. Suicide murderers are in a rush to heaven, which they picture as a discount whorehouse. If that's not sufficiently depraved, behold the ghoulish spectacle of a mother celebrating the death of her own (terrorist) child—a brand new hero by dint of the misery he inflicted on other mothers and other children. Theirs is the party of death indeed.

We understand our mission. The champions of life must defeat the champions of death.[9]

Americans must understand all of this—for our own sake, and for that of the world. Victory in the war against global jihadism will require sacrifice; that is obvious. What is perhaps not so obvious is the nature of the sacrifice required to deserve victory in the war against this particular threat: the sacrifice of our addiction to instant gratification and immediate success.

President George W. Bush's successor will quickly learn that there is no escape from the burden of American leadership. That president, whoever he or she may be, should see that burden as an opportunity. So should the American people. In this war we did not seek, but which we must fight and in which we must prevail, there is opportunity for national self-renewal, and opportunity to serve freedom's cause and the cause of life throughout the world.

Afterword

The last two years of the Bush administration saw some significant successes in the war against jihadism.

The Sunni Awakening in western Iraq's Anbar Province, the progress made throughout the rest of Iraq under General David Petraeus's counterinsurgency strategy, and the resolution shown by Iraqi leaders across the ethnic and religious divides that had previously dominated local politics all contributed to a major defeat for al-Qaeda in Iraq. And that defeat, in turn, did serious damage to al-Qaeda's image of invincibility throughout the world. As it left office on January 20, 2009, the Bush administration could also point with justifiable satisfaction to the fact that every effort by jihadist terrorism to strike the American homeland since 9/11 had been interdicted or frustrated—something no one imagined possible when contemplating the smoldering ruins of the Twin Towers, the gaping hole in the Pentagon, and the wreckage of United Flight 93 in mid-September

2001. There were even indications that the world economic crisis of 2008–2009 was having at least one positive effect: like everyone else, terrorists and their state sponsors had fewer financial resources at their disposal.

Yet the success of the Petraeus surge in Iraq–which John McCain had supported and Barack Obama had opposed–had a curious political effect in the United States. By taking Iraq (and, by extension, the broader war against jihadism) off the table as a key 2008 issue, Obama benefitted immensely from the success of a policy he had opposed at little political risk to himself. McCain's candidacy, on the other hand, suffered from the success of a policy he had helped drive through the Congress at considerable political risk. By helping prevent an American defeat in Iraq that would have been calamitous for U.S. anti-terrorism policy, John McCain made it easier for Americans to dismiss him as a man of the past while reposing their political hopes in his inexperienced opponent. There are indeed many ironies in the fire.

Media common wisdom and the Democratic congressional leadership both continued to treat the entire Bush foreign policy as an unmitigated disaster throughout the lengthy 2008 political cycle. The facts, however, indicated that, at least in some respects, the United States was in a stronger position in the war against jihadist terrorism as the Obama administration took office. This was in no small part because the U.S. military, which seems to have a greater capacity for self-correction than any other large institution in our society, had learned valuable lessons about this new kind of war, and had put those lessons to good use. (To take the most obvious example: those responsible for the lives of American boots-on-the-ground in Iraq had faced the fact that a "small footprint" strategy aimed at keeping U.S. forces in the background after the fall of the Saddam Hussein regime had failed, and had in fact exacerbated inter-ethnic and interreligious tensions in Iraq to the point where the country was on the verge of falling apart. Enter David Petraeus.) Some of those lessons in counterinsurgency will doubtless serve the United States well on other battlefronts in the war against jihadism. Yet while the U.S. military showed commendable strategic flexibility under the pressure of potential failure, the government continued to suffer from many of the disabilities outlined in this book throughout the latter Bush administration years. Those failures of perception and analysis pose a serious challenge to the new American leadership and to President Obama personally.

GOVERNMENTAL MYOPIA, UNCORRECTED

Perhaps the most striking of these disabilities is the continued refusal of senior American officials to describe the enemy in this new kind of war accurately and dispassionately.

As the Bush administration gave way to the Obama administration, the Department of State, the Department of Defense, and the Central Intelligence Agency all remained allergic to any discussion of the religious dimension of Islamist terrorism, to the point where the more inquiring minds in those key agencies read this book as a form of *samizdat* throughout 2008. The January 2009 issue of *Foreign Affairs* carried what was regarded throughout the defense and foreign policy communities as a seminal article, laying out a post–Bush administration approach to defense strategy and procurement. Written by Secretary of Defense Robert Gates (who had agreed to stay in his office through the beginning of the Obama administration) and entitled "A Balanced Strategy: Reprogramming the Pentagon for a New Age," the article had not a single word to say about political Islamism, jihadism, or the distorted religious passions that had done so much in the previous decade and a half to shape the security environment in which the Defense Department must operate. President Obama's extended hand to the Muslim world during his inaugural address and his comments in an al-Arabiya television interview during his first week in office—in which he suggested that the Islamic world and the West could return to some putative previous condition of harmony and stability—similarly ignored the internal, theological and self-generating sources of jihadism described above, as did his June 2009 speech to "the Muslim world" in Cairo. Moreover, by seeming to place the primary responsibility for current tensions between Islam and "the rest" on western (and specifically American) ineptitudes and mistakes, the new president's remarks likely reinforced the debilitating tendency in the Arab Islamic world to blame its problems on "the other." Furthermore, in his al-Arabiya interview, President Obama failed to remind his Arabic-speaking viewers that American blood and treasure had liberated Muslims from various forms of despotism in the Balkans, in Afghanistan, and in Iraq over the past two decades. Moreover, Obama's implication that the West, through what he evidently regarded as mistaken policies, had warped Arab Islamic political culture may have inadvertently reinforced yet another crippling mental habit in that world: its tendency to think of itself as a victim, not a protagonist, of history.

Thus one of the signal failures of the Bush administration—almost entirely unremarked during the 2008 campaign and in the mainstream media—was that it did not compel the principal foreign, defense, and intelligence agencies of the U.S. government to confront their secularist assumptions about the incapacity of religious conviction to shape world politics. In the years after 9/11, as in the decade before, those assumptions continued to distort these agencies' understanding of religious passions as one of the principal dynamics of the twenty-first-century world; and that myopia seemed poised to continue to distort the government's vision far into the future, for by all empirical counts the world is becoming more, not less, religious. One hopes for improvement here, but it seems unlikely that those distortions of perception will be addressed and repaired in an Obama administration staffed, in the main, by men and women of a secular cast of mind similar to that of the permanent national security bureaucracy. Yet removing those secularist intellectual blinders in order to understand how religious conviction and passion shape world politics in the twenty-first century is the *sine qua non* of sound policy and strategy in the war against jihadism. Unless the default positions on this question are reset at the Department of State, the Department of Defense, and the CIA, the United States will continue to be disarmed intellectually in a war it can neither avoid nor afford to lose.

A NEW INTERRELIGIOUS DIALOGUE?

While the U.S. government remained more or less blind to religion's role in the world at the end of the first decade of the twenty-first century, the world's two largest religious communities—the Catholic Church and Islam—engaged in several probes toward a new, and just perhaps more serious, form of interreligious dialogue. The credit for initiating these new processes must go to Pope Benedict XVI, whose much-deplored Regensburg Lecture of September 2006 triggered shock waves of considerable force throughout the worlds-within-worlds of Islam. As a result, new initiatives were launched, both by the so-called "Group of 136" (an ad hoc aggregation of religious leaders, scholars, and governmental functionaries from throughout the Islamic world) and by King Abdullah of Saudi Arabia. As of early 2009, neither of these projects had produced any substantial advances. Nonetheless, they had sharpened the understanding of at least some of the dialogue participants as to what had to be on the agenda of an interreligious dialogue worth engaging—such as the question of religious freedom and its institutional embodiment in the laws and practices by which states manage the often-complex relationship between religious and political authority.

Here, too, the primary credit must go to Benedict XVI, who kept insisting, throughout 2006, 2007, and 2008, that any serious interreligious dialogue with Islam must focus on two central issues that modern political life had rendered unavoidable for believers in the God of Abraham. The first issue was the defense of religious freedom as a basic human right that can be grasped by reason. The second issue was the theological and philosophical justification for the distinction between religious and political authority in a justly ordered twenty-first-century state. In addition, the Pope suggested, Christians in the West (and the West as a political culture) must be able to demonstrate to Muslims that the institutional separation of religious and political authority does not necessarily lead to state-sponsored atheism, which is a misapprehension from which many Muslims, and indeed many Arab Christians, suffer.

In a 2008 lecture at Cambridge University, one of Benedict's key advisors on Islamic affairs, the German Jesuit Christian Troll, outlined a template of issues and questions that ought to frame the interreligious dialogue of the immediate future—a template that should be of interest to public officials as well as scholars of religion (the passages in quotation marks below are from Father Troll's lecture):

1. *Liberation through conversion and repentance:* Can Christians and Muslims speak frankly to each other about the temptation, common to adherents of both faiths, to so degrade the "other" that he or she becomes an object of persecution, even persecution in the name of God? Is it enough for Christians and Muslims to be instructed by their faiths in the dual commandment of love of God and love of neighbor? Is such instruction sufficient to overcome the hu-

man propensity for wickedness toward the "other?"
Or is something more required—that is, do Christians and Muslims "share an awareness of our need
to be liberated by God into the freedom of His gift of
love"? Are we agreed that we must all repent of the
times when coercion has been used to advance the
cause of God? Is self-criticism part of the spiritual
self-awareness of both Christians and Muslims?

2. *Faith and reason:* Is it possible for Christians
and Muslims to study their sacred texts with a piety
informed by rigorous historical and literary analysis? Is it possible to create a "critical Christian-Mus-
lim scholarship marked by the will to understand
out of love?" Is it a betrayal of faith to apply modern
scholarly methods to study and discussion of the
origins and character of the Bible and the Qur'an?

3. *Human rights:* Do we agree that God himself
has inscribed human rights "into the nature of
man?" Are we agreed that "human rights and divine rights cannot be played off one against the
other"? If by "human rights" we mean the recognition and legal protection of the basic, minimal conditions under which "the human dignity . . . due to
the human person as a creature of God" is protected, then can we agree that "to recognize and respect human rights is nothing but obedience to the
will of God"? Is the protection of human rights thus
a fulfillment of the dual commandment of love of
God and love of neighbor (which was the ground

on which the "Group of 136" sought to build the post-Regensburg dialogue)? If "Islam" means "submission to the will of God," and if respect for the dignity of the human person is of the will of God, then does Islam by its very nature require Muslims to recognize basic human rights? (And if that is not the case, why isn't it?)

4. *Religious freedom:* Doesn't love of neighbor require (and as a religious obligation, not merely a practical political accommodation) respect and legal protection for the religious convictions of others, so long as those convictions do not compromise the common good? Do Muslims agree that that principle holds even if Muslims regard what the "other" believes is false? Can we agree that the institutional separation of religious and political authority is good for the state (because it prevents the state from sacralizing itself) and for religion (because it prevents the misuse of religion for political purposes and creates social space for faith and for the workings of conscience)? Christians now recognize that the attempt to create Christian states was a failure that involved "great costs on all sides." Are Muslims prepared to recognize that the attempt to create Islamic states will likely lead to the same bad results, for both justice and faith?

5. *Violence and reciprocity:* Can Islam understand its faith in such a way that Muslims reject violence in the name of God, both in terms of a cleansing of

conscience about the past and as a commitment to the future? Can this commitment extend to those who leave the House of Islam for other faiths? The Qur'an teaches that no one may be forced to believe; can Muslims agree that that principle "only comes to fruition if it guarantees the freedom also to abandon the faith, to understand it differently, or even to despise it"? Can Christians and Muslims both agree that "it is only God's affair to judge the weight of such matters"?

At first blush, such questions may seem far removed from the concerns and responsibilities of governments. And it is true that governments would be singularly blunt instruments in facilitating a dialogue based on such a template; the leadership here must come from elsewhere. Yet unless western governments understand that jihadism is one lethal by-product of an intra-Islamic civil war that has been focused for decades on precisely the questions in Troll's template, the West will, to say it once again, have failed to understand the nature of the enemy, his motivations, and the variety of instruments required to defeat him.

A QUESTION OF PERSPECTIVE

It is primarily the responsibility of those religious leaders and scholars engaged in the post-Regensburg interreligious dialogue to guide the conversation back to the kinds of questions proposed by Christian Troll, despite various degrees of Muslim resistance. There are, however, things governments can do to support such efforts. Take three examples, from misguided government actions undertaken since this book was first published.

The U.S. Department of Homeland Security's strictures on avoiding the word "jihad" in describing what it is we are confronting would be rejected as foolish in themselves and as bad guides to good policy. Denying the truth of what it is we face, and why our enemies hate us, not only reinforces the effects of jihadist mendacity; just as importantly, it undercuts the efforts of Muslim reformers to challenge, and ultimately marginalize, the radicals in their religious community.

Then there is western Europe, where governments continue to make both overt and tacit concessions to shari'a law on matters ranging from marriage to education to the protection of basic civil liberties. Such concessions not only create legal chaos and undermine democratic confidence in the rule of law, but they also reinforce local Islamists and jihadists at the expense of those Muslims who are trying to find an authentically Islamic way to live under the conditions of political modernity. Such concessions must stop.

Finally, there is America's neighbor to the north,

where civil liberties are crumbling under the combined threat of Islamist pressures and multiculturalist shibboleths. Despite their noble name, Canada's "Human Rights Commissions" are extra-judicial star chambers which try to punish the exercise of free speech and freedom of the press when Islamists and jihadists take offense at what is said or printed or broadcast. These exercises in political correctness–which can cost their victims tens of thousands of dollars in legal bills, even if the alleged offender is acquitted–do nothing for religious freedom, rightly understood; at the same time, just as in western Europe, they encourage Islamist radicals to continue their pressures even as they disempower Islamic reformers. If Canada is to remain a land of freedom, these star chambers must be reined in–or, even better, abolished.

Thus the great change still required of virtually all western governments is a change of strategic perspective. It is essential to the security of the West that those Muslims who seek an accommodation with political modernity while retaining their core religious convictions win out over those Muslims who violently reject political modernity as incompatible with their notion of their faith. Yet the West will not be able to offer even modest help in shifting the internal balance of power within the Islamic world if the West does not recognize that appeasement, either in the form of concessions to shari'a law or in the form of legally imposed political correctness, does not work with jihadists. On the contrary, appeasement reinforces the hand of those Islamists determined to defeat political modernity.

Appeasement, alas, remains a grave temptation in a West in which influential sectors of opinion (and many government leaders) continue to believe, against all the available evidence, that the problem of jihadism would simply evaporate, if: *if* there were an independent Palestinian state; *if* further concessions were made in western domestic law to shari'a courts; *if* the West would only concede that the history of its interaction with the Islamic world is emblematically captured by the Crusades and colonialism. That temptation, in turn, reflects a lack of western self-confidence in the West's capacity to defend its commitments to civility, tolerance, human rights, and the rule of law with the arts of reason and persuasion.

The challenge to the West thus remains precisely what it was when this small primer on the war against jihadism was first published. This most rigorously self-critical of civilizations must recover its nerve, its sense of proportion, and its appreciation of its own best political instincts if it is to secure the future of freedom in the face of the jihadist challenge. Victory in the war against jihadism must be sought on many fronts, ranging from combat zones throughout the world to intelligence gathering and analysis to economic restructuring.

The path to victory in the war against jihadism begins at home, however. And it begins in our own minds and hearts.

G.W.
Washington, D.C.
July 4, 2009

Acknowledgments

The argument of this book was first outlined in the sixth William E. Simon Lecture, which I delivered for the Ethics and Public Policy Center in Washington, D.C., in January 2007. I am grateful to the board and staff of the William E. Simon Foundation for their sponsorship of this annual lecture, with special thanks to William E. Simon, Jr., J. Peter Simon, James Piereson, and Sheila Mulcahy for their encouragement and support over many years.

Elements of the argument appeared in *First Things* and *Commentary*, and I thank Father Richard John Neuhaus and Neal Kozodoy for opening the pages of their distinguished journals to my work.

Many friends and colleagues were helpful in sharing critical comments, recommendations, and materials as I was preparing this book: Elliott Abrams, Father Joseph Alobaidi, O.P., Robert Andrews, Paul Belien, Rémi Brague, Yigal Carmon, Michael A. Casey, Michael Cromartie, Father Joseph Augustine DiNoia, O.P., William Doino Jr., William Donohue, Jean Duchesne, Philip Eaton, Thomas F. Farr, Hillel

Fradkin, Edward R. Grant, Jr., Mary Habeck, Daniel
Henninger, James Turner Johnson, Laura Johnston,
Max Kampelman, Leon Kass, James Lacey, Ernest W.
Lefever, Christopher Levenick, Stephen Lewarne,
Jon Meacham, Gilbert Meilaender, Menahem Mil-
son, John Mueller, Michael Novak, Father Edward T.
Oakes, S.J., Robert C. Odle, Jr., Charles Paternina,
Robert Satloff, Stephen Schwartz, Father William
Stetson, John Vinocur, Peter H. Wehner, Joseph R.
Wood, and R. James Woolsey. It should go without
saying, but I'll say it anyway, that I am solely respon-
sible for the book's argument.

M. Edward Whelan III has proven an outstanding
president of the Ethics and Public Policy Center; I
thank him for his work in expanding the Center's
range of interests and influence, and for his personal
support and wise counsel. Stephen White did an ex-
emplary job of research and kept my office running
smoothly. I am, as always, deeply grateful to the
donors who make the Catholic Studies Program of
EPPC possible.

Thanks, too, to my literary agent, Loretta Barrett,
and to Bill Barry of Doubleday, both of whom saw
the point, quickly.

Joan Weigel, Gwyneth Susil, Monica Weigel, and
Stephen Weigel all had interesting comments on the
original lecture, and I thank them for their interest,
love, and support.

I first met a young Australian priest named George
Pell in the summer of 1967, when he came to my

home parish in Baltimore prior to his graduate studies at Oxford. Over the past forty years, our friendship and collaboration have deepened. We spoke at length about the post-9/11 world during our time together in Rome in October 2001. That conversation has continued ever since, and so it is a great pleasure to dedicate this book to an old and cherished friend, the cardinal archbishop of Sydney.

> G.W.
> Washington, D.C.
> Commemoration of St. George
> April 23, 2007

Notes

INTRODUCTION

1. See Lawrence Wright, *The Looming Tower: Al-Qaeda and the Road to 9/11* (New York: Knopf, 2006), pp. 356–359.

2. Ibid., p. 6.

3. See Walter Laqueur, *No End to War: Terrorism in the Twenty-First Century* (New York: Continuum, 2004), pp. 9, 14, 24. Professor Laqueur also notes the proximate historical origins of this new form of terrorist fanaticism:

There were not a few unstable personalities among the nineteenth-century terrorists, especially the Anarchists and the Russians, but there were few paranoiacs among them. On the other hand, persecution mania plays an important part in the new terrorism.

The term "fanaticism" comes from the Latin *fanum* (a holy place), but acquired early on the meaning of being possessed. It has frequently been described by theologians and historians of religion, whereas psychiatrists and psychologists have often shied away from investigating the phenomenon. A workable definition has been provided by Adolf Hitler in *Mein Kampf*; more than any other modern leader

Hitler invoked fanaticism as an essential element of the Nazi movement.

Hitler noted that the mobilization of the masses could never be achieved by "half-hearted statements and actions" but only by total lack of any (human) consideration and the fanatical, relentless pursuit of the goal. The enemy had to be smashed and destroyed; he was not just wrong, he was always totally wrong. (p. 25)

4. Victor Davis Hanson, "War-Making and the Machinery of War," *Commentary*, December 2006, p. 46.

5. Which would not, alas, be all that difficult to do. See, for example, Peter D. Zimmerman and Jeffrey G. Lewis, "The Bomb in the Backyard," *Foreign Policy*, November–December 2006, pp. 33–39, which describes how al-Qaeda or a similar organization could assemble a nuclear weapon on U.S. soil, and then deploy it.

6. See Samuel P. Huntington, *The Clash of Civilizations and the Remaking of World Order* (New York: Simon & Schuster, 1997). As Dr. Huntington notes with some chagrin, the article on which this book was based "had a generally ignored question mark in its title" (p. 13).

7. On this crucial, point, see Charles Krauthammer, "Past the Apogee: America Under Pressure," Foreign Policy Research Institute E-Notes, December 2006, available at http://www.fpri.org.

8. On North Waziristan, see Robert D. Kaplan, *Imperial Grunts: On the Ground with the American Military, from Mongolia to the Philippines to Iraq and Beyond* (New York: Vintage Books, 2006), p. 236.

9. Cited in Mark Steyn, "The Apathy of Defeat," *Western Standard*, September 25, 2006.

PART ONE: UNDERSTANDING THE ENEMY

Lesson 1

1. See Richard Dawkins, *The God Delusion* (New York: Houghton Mifflin, 2006); Daniel Dennett, *Breaking the Spell: Religion as a Natural Phenomenon* (New York: Viking, 2006); Christopher Hitchens, *God Is Not Great: How Religion Poisons Everything* (New York: Twelve Books, 2007); and Sam Harris, *Letter to a Christian Nation* (New York: Knopf, 2006).

Lesson 2

1. See David Novak, *Jewish-Christian Dialogue: A Jewish Justification* (New York: Oxford University Press, 1989).

2. Alain Besançon, "What Kind of Religion Is Islam?" *Commentary*, May 2004, p. 45. On Abraham as neither Jew nor Christian, but rather a Muslim, see Qur'an 3:67. On the noncrucifixion of Jesus, see Qur'an 4:157. On the Quranic view of the Trinity as composed of God, Mary, and Jesus, see Qur'an 5:116.

3. In *Islam and the West: The Making of an Image* (Oxford, UK: Oneworld Publications, 1997), a study widely regarded in interreligious circles as a classic, British scholar Norman Daniel is at pains to challenge aspects of the "image" of Islam he finds in Christian commentators like St. John Damascene. Still, on this point, Daniel writes as follows about the religious and cultural circumstances from which Islam was born:

Thus, in the less fabulous writers a fairly consistent picture of ancient Arabia develops: wild, barbaric, a simple and illiterate population, unorganized, ungoverned, at least in Medina; exposed to outside influences from the East Roman Empire, but penetrated rather by refugees from ecclesiastical conflict than by orthodox missionaries. Such unofficial missions succeeded, not among the superior mercantile community of Mecca, but among the rustics of Medina whose Jewish neighbors had already influenced them. Muhammad was the natural product of this world.... This is not a ridiculously unhistorical picture, as is, on the contrary, that which imagined any considerable acceptance of orthodox Christianity in the Arabia into which Muhammad was born. (p. 106)

On the complex situation of pre-Islamic Arabia, see also Reza Aslan, *No God But God: The Origins, Evolution, and Future of Islam* (New York: Random House, 2006), pp. 6–13.

4. Aquinas's critique, which is set in the context of his discussion of faith and reason, may be found in the *Summa Contra Gentiles* I:6:4 (South Bend, IN: University of Notre Dame Press, 1975).

5. See Qur'an 3:85, on the eternal loss of those, including the "People of the Book," who do not become Muslims.

6. Classic Islam teaches that Jews and Christians tampered with the texts of the Hebrew Bible and the New Testament in order to remove references to the Prophet of Islam, whose coming was foretold, according to the Qur'an (3:81, 7:157, 61:6), in the original versions of the sacred texts of Jews and Christians. See F. E. Peters, *Judaism, Christianity, Islam*, vol. 2, *The Word and the Law and the People of God* (Princeton, NJ: Princeton University Press, 1990), pp. 33–37, for the exposition of this claim by an eleventh-century Muslim theologian, Juwayni, in a book called *The Noble Healing*, and pp. 348–351 for a parallel commentary on the relevant

Qur'anic verses by the twelfth-century commentator Za-
makhshari.

7. Huntington, *Clash of Civilizations*, pp. 254–258.

8. Bernard Lewis, *The Muslim Discovery of Europe*
(New York: Norton, 2001), p. 302.

9. Ibid., pp. 33–34.

10. Ibid., p. 46. See also Ian W. Toll, *Six Frigates: The
Epic History of the Founding of the U.S. Navy* (New York:
Norton, 2006).

11. Cited in Lewis, *Muslim Discovery of Europe*, p. 41.

12. M. A. S. Abdel Haleem, "Introduction," in *The
Qur'an* (New York: Oxford University Press, 2005), p. ix.

In *Islam and the West*, Norman Daniel describes the distinctive character of the Qur'an, as Muslims understand it,
in these terms:

> The Qur'an has no parallel outside Islam. Christians have
> sometimes seen it as equivalent to the Bible. They have not
> always realized that the Qur'an describes itself . . . as copied
> from a heavenly prototype, so that it is really unlike any-
> thing known to Christianity. . . . The Qur'an in Islam is very
> nearly what Christ is in Christianity: the Word of God, the
> whole expression of revelation. For the most Bible-loving
> Protestant or Catholic, the Bible derives its significance from
> Christ; but Muhammad derives his from the Qur'an. In their
> failure to realize this [westerners have] persistently con-
> trasted Christ and Muhammad, and nothing marks more
> clearly the distance between Islamic and European thought.
> (p. 53)

13. Second Vatican Council, Dogmatic Constitution on
Divine Revelation (*Dei Verbum*), 11.

14. See Peters, *Word and the Law*, pp. 40–41, for an exposition of the several Qur'anic texts involving the Qur'an's description of its origins. One of the key texts is Qur'an 10:37–39: "Nor could this Qur'an have been devised by anyone other than God. It is a confirmation of what has been revealed before and an explanation of the Scripture—let there be no doubt about if–from the Lord of the Worlds. Or do they say, 'He [i.e., Muhammad] has devised it?' Say, 'Produce a sura like it, and call on anyone you can beside God if you are telling the truth.' But they are denying what they cannot comprehend–its prophecy has yet to be fulfilled for them. In the same way, those before them refused to believe–see what was the end of those evildoers."

15. Abu Hamza al-Masri, cited in Mary Habeck, *Knowing the Enemy: Jihadist Ideology and the War on Terror* (New Haven: Yale University Press, 2006), p. 43.

16. As one of France's leading scholars of medieval Islamic philosophy, Rémi Brague, writes,

The female veil provides a typical example. It appears in both the Qur'an and the New Testament, as has often been remarked. In the Qur'an it is Allah who is speaking and who commands believing women to "draw their veils over their bosoms" and "cast their outer garments over their persons." In the New Testament there is a fairly long and fairly obscure passage in which Paul, too, tells women to be veiled when they pray (I Corinthians 11:3–26). The two recommendations are thus quite close in their content, but the text of the epistle is not a command from God but counsel from Paul. We can interpret Paul's intention as a desire for women to be decently dressed, advice that can be adapted according to the criteria in force in a given place and time. If, on the contrary, Allah in person is the author of the injunctions in the Qur'an, it is hard to see how any interpretation could go beyond and explication of the length or opacity of the veil or an examination of words: exactly what parts of the body and what sort of "garments" are involved? (*The Law of God: The Philosophial History of an Idea* [Chicago: University of Chicago Press, 2007], pp. 73–74.)

17. Besançon, "What Kind of Religion Is Islam?" p. 45.

18. On this last point, see Daniel, *Islam and the West*, p. 185.

19. John Paul II, *Crossing the Threshold of Hope* (New York: Knopf, 1995), pp. 92, 93.

20. Lewis, *Muslim Discovery of Europe*, pp. 39, 53, 61.

21. Islam's radical stress on the unicity (oneness) of God, which Islam sharply distinguishes from the Christian Trinitarian concept of God, may also help explain the differing success each religion has had in creating societies characterized by a healthy, vibrant social pluralism. The Trinitarian God of Christianity—"Emmanuel," or "God With Us"—is an idea of the God of Abraham that makes possible God's intimate relationship to the world ("How could God be with us if the word *with* were not part and parcel of his own being and life?" as the Swiss theologian Hans Urs von Balthasar once asked). It also makes possible an instinct for the pluralism of orderly relations among different persons in the world (because the Trinitarian God is in himself a "being with," we must "be with" others)—or so it might be speculated. See Hans Urs von Balthasar, *You Crown the Year with Your Goodness* (San Francisco: Ignatius Press, 1989), p. 141.

22. On Islam's "fusion of religious and temporal authority" and "millenarian imperial experience," see Efraim Karsh, *Islamic Imperialism: A History* (New Haven, CT: Yale University Press, 2006), pp. 18, 5. For Berger on pluralism: see "Religion in a Globalizing World" at http://pewforum.org/events/print.php?EventID=136. On *dhimmis,* see Bat Ye'or, *The Decline of Eastern Christianity Under Islam: From Jihad to Dhimmitude* (Madison, NJ: Fairleigh Dickinson University Press, 1996).

Karsh's description of dhimmitude is instructive:

> The "protected communities" (the term was originally applied to Christians and Jews, but was subsequently expanded to other non-Muslim groups) were allowed to keep their properties and to practice their religions in return for a distinctly inferior status that was institutionalized over time. They had to pay special taxes (regularized at a later stage as land tax, *kharaj,* and the more humiliating poll tax, *jizya*) and suffered from social indignities and at times open persecution. Their religious activities outside the churches and synagogues were curtailed, the ringing of bells was forbidden, the construction of new church buildings prohibited, and the proselytizing of Muslims was made a capital offense punishable by death. Jews and Christians had to wear distinctive clothes to distinguish them from their Muslim lords, could ride only donkeys, not horses, could not marry Muslim women, had to vacate their seats whenever Muslims wanted them, were excluded from positions of power, and so on and so forth. (pp. 25–26)

This description is a useful rejoinder to those apologists who claim that Islam was never spread by the sword: although conversions to Islam were occasionally effected at sword point, what was spread by the sword was, in the main (and at first), the Arabic empire. Once Muslims had seized power, however, and given their understanding that the ideal within the House of Islam is "a single community, governed by a single state, headed by a single sovereign" (Lewis, *Muslim Discovery of Europe*, p. 61), they decreed and enforced laws that made conversion to Islam advantageous, humiliated Jews and Christians, and, as noted above, made conversion from Islam punishable in principle by death. These dynamics of *dhimmitude*, rather than mass conversion at the risk of death with a scimitar at one's throat, help explain why Egypt, once an overwhelmingly Christian country, became, within a short period after its conquest by Islam, a Muslim country.

23. Bernard Lewis, *The Crisis of Islam: Holy War and Unholy Terror* (London: Phoenix, 2003), p. 5.

24. See George Weigel, *The Cube and the Cathedral: Europe, America, and Politics Without God* (New York: Basic Books, 2005).

25. Besançon, "What Kind of Religion Is Islam?" p. 42.

26. Besançon points this out in "What Kind of Religion Is Islam?" p. 47, assigning responsibility to the French Catholic scholar Louis Massignon (1883–1962) and his disciples.

Lesson 3

1. Richard John Neuhaus, "The Regensburg Moment," *First Things*, November 2006, p. 68.

2. Ibid., pp. 68–69.

Lesson 4

1. Bernard Lewis sums up, in *What Went Wrong? The Clash Between Islam and Modernity in the Middle East* (New York: Harper Perennial, 2002):

> At the peak of Islamic power, there was only one civilization that was comparable in the level, quality, and variety of achievement; that was of course China. But Chinese civilization remains essentially local, limited to one region, East Asia, and to one racial group. . . . Islam in contrast created a world civilization, polyethnic, multiracial, international, one might even say intercontinental.
>
> For centuries the world view and self-view of Muslims seemed well grounded. Islam represented the greatest military power on earth—its armies, at the very same time, were invading Europe and Africa, India and China. It was the foremost economic power in the world, trading in a range of commodities through a far-flung network of commerce and communications in Asia, Europe, and Africa; importing slaves and gold from Africa, slaves and wool from Europe, and exchanging a variety of foodstuffs, materials, and manufactures with the civilized countries of Asia. It had achieved the highest level so far in human history in the arts and sciences of civilization. Inheriting the knowledge and skills of the ancient Middle East, of Greece and of Persia, it added to them several important innovations from outside, such as the use and manufacture of paper from China and decimal positional numbering from India. It is difficult to imagine modern literature or science without the one or the other. It was in the Islamic Middle East that Indian numbers were for the first time incorporated in the inherited body of mathematical learning. From the Middle

East they were transmitted to the West, where they are still known as Arabic numerals, honoring not those who invented them but those who first brought them to Europe. To this rich inheritance scholars and scientists in the Islamic world added an immensely important contribution through their own observations, experiments, and ideas. In most of the arts and sciences of civilization, medieval Europe was a pupil and in a sense a dependent of the Islamic world, relying on Arabic versions even for many otherwise unknown Greek works.

And then suddenly, the relationship changed. (pp. 6–7)

2. Frederick Copleston, S.J., *History of Philosophy*, vol. 2, *Augustine to Scotus* (Westminster, MD: Newman Press, 1957), p. 196.

3. Ibid., pp. 186, 197–199.

4. Lewis, *Muslim Discovery of Europe*, p. 51. Lewis continues:

The Muslim world had its own discoveries, as the expansion of the Arab Muslim armies brought them to civilizations as remote and as diverse as Europe, India, and China. It also had its renaissance, in the recovery of Greek and, to a lesser extent, Persian learning in the early Islamic centuries. But these events did not coincide, and they were not accompanied by any loosening of theological bonds. The Islamic renaissance came when the expansion of Islam had ceased and the counterattack of Christendom was beginning. The intellectual struggle of ancients and moderns, of theologians and philosophers, ended in an overwhelming and enduring victory of the first over the second. This confirmed the Muslim world in the belief in its own self-sufficiency and superiority as the one repository of the true faith and–which for Muslims meant the same thing–of the civilized way of life. (p. 300)

5. Cited in Lewis, *Crisis of Islam*, p. 99. This was the first of four "Arab Human Development" reports, issued in 2002, 2003, 2005, and 2007. The first report noted the correlation between intellectual stagnation and political repression in the Arab Islamic world.

6. Lewis, *Muslim Discovery of Europe*, p. 27.

7. Habeck, *Knowing the Enemy*, p. 21.

8. Laqueur, *No End to War*, p. 85.

9. See Habeck, *Knowing the Enemy*, pp. 23–26.

10. Hasan al-Banna, "Between Yesterday and Today," cited in Habek, *Knowing the Enemy*, p. 30.

11. Laqueur, *No End to War*, p. 32; Habeck, *Knowing the Enemy*, pp. 30–32. Hasan al-Banna's *Jihad* may be found at www.youngmuslims.ca/online_library/books/jihad.

12. Wright, *Looming Tower*, p. 8.

13. Ibid., pp. 22, 10.

14. Laqueur, *No End to War*, p. 33.

15. Habeck, *Knowing the Enemy*, pp. 35–36, 66.

16. Laqueur, *No End to War*, p. 36. Qutb's *Milestones* may be found at www.masmn.org/documents/Books/Syed_Qutb/Milestones/index.htm.

17. See Middle East Media Research Institute, "Saudi Government-Appointed Executioner Interview Discusses His Calling and Demonstrates His Weapous and Methods," MEMRI Special Dispatch No. 1374, December 1, 2006, available at http://memri.org.

18. Wright, *Looming Tower*, pp. 24, 107.

19. See M. A. Casey, "Democracy and the Thin Veneer of Civilization," *Quadrant*, November 2006, p. 38; Fouad Ajami, "The New Boys of Terror," *U.S. News & World Report*, October 1, 2006; Victor Davis Hanson, "The Brink of Madness," *National Review Online*, August 4, 2006, available at http://www.nationalreview.com; Wright, *Looming Tower*, p. 231.

20. Wright, *Looming Tower*, p. 127.

Lesson 5

1. Laqueur, *No End to War*, pp. 49, 51.

2. Ibid., pp. 54–55.

3. Wright, *Looming Tower*, p. 285. Something of the devotion bin Laden drew from his followers can be discerned in a 2007 al-Arabiya television interview with his former bodyguard, Nasser Al-Bahri, in which Al-Bahri said, "I place Sheikh Osama on the same level as my father, and I love him perhaps even more than my father" (Middle East Media Research Institute, MEMRI Special Dispatch No. 1611, June 6, 2007).

4. Ibid., pp. 319–320.

5. Ibid., p. 331.

6. Bin Laden's declaration may be found at www.outpost-of-freedom.com/opf980830a.htm.

7. Fouad Ajami, *The Foreigner's Gift: The Americans, the Arabs, and the Iraqis in Iraq* (New York: Free Press, 2006), p. xii.

8. Laqueur, *No End to War*, p. 15.

9. Ibid., p. 17.

10. Ajami, *Foreigner's Gift*, p. 151.

11. Laqueur, *No End to War*, p. 212.

12. Cited in Peter Wehner, "The War Against Global Jihadism," www.realclearpolitics.com. January 8, 2007.

Lesson 6

1. Besançon, "What Kind of Religion Is Islam?" p. 48.

2. The full text of the Regensburg Lecture, including the supporting scholarly apparatus, can be found at www.vatican.va.

3. The full text of the "Open Letter" can be found at www.islamicamagazine.com/letter. The defensiveness of Aref Ali Nayed's article, "A Muslim's Commentary on Benedict XVI's Regensburg Lecture" (*Islamica* 18 [2006], pp. 46–54), inadvertently but usefully demonstrates just how difficult it will be to initiate and sustain a serious dialogue, given the accumulated psychological detritus of the centuries and the Arab disinclination to engage respectful challenge and critique. This is perhaps one reason why some scholars suggest constructing the needed dialogue, initially, in parts of the Islamic world outside the Arabic cultural sphere.

4. The two most prominent figures who did not sign the "Open Letter" were the head of Al-Azhar University in Cairo, Sheikh Muhammad Tantawi, and the Egyptian-born jurist Yussef el Qaradawi. In *No End to War*, Walter Laqueur describes aspects of these men's jurisprudence as follows:

In our time, various religious dignitaries in Egypt and Saudi Arabia have opposed suicide terrorism, but others—such as the Mufti of Jerusalem and Palestine—have justified it as *shahada* (martyrdom). Yet others have taken a middle way, regarding attacks against enemy soldiers as permissible, but attacks against civilians as not. Some have favored suicide attacks against the "Zionist [occupiers]" in Palestine but not against fellow Muslims. Sheikh Muhammad Tantawi, head of Al Azhar in Cairo, said on one occasion that all Israelis— men, women, and children—were forces of occupation and therefore legitimate targets of suicide bombers. But on another occasion he said that no Muslim should blow himself up in the midst of children and women but only among aggressors, among soldiers. Yussef el Qaradawi, the TV sheikh of the Al Jezira network, famous in the whole Arab world, also declared suicide terrorism the highest form of jihad and therefore very commendable. (pp. 71–72)

5. These unfortunate trends in reportage on the Regensburg Lecture in particular, and Catholicism and Islam in general, are summarized in one particularly uncomprehending article by Jane Kramer, "The Pope and Islam," which appeared in the April 2, 2007, issue of the *New Yorker*. Kramer's essay, replete with factual errors and tendentious analysis, does have the (unintended) merit of giving a clear glimpse into the mental worlds of professional interreligious dialoguers and appeasement-minded Catholic intellectuals and activists.

6. The relevant sections of Benedict's address to the Curia were these:

In a dialogue to be intensified with Islam, we must bear in mind the fact that the Muslim world today is finding itself faced with an urgent task. This task is very similar to the one that was imposed upon Christians since the Enlightenment, and to which the Second Vatican Council II, as the fruit of long and difficult research, found real solutions for the Catholic Church. . . .

It is a question of the attitude that the community of the faithful must adopt in the face of the convictions and demands that were strengthened in the Enlightenment.

On the one hand, one must counter a dictatorship of positivist reason that excludes God from the life of the community and from public organizations. . . .

On the other hand, one must welcome the true conquests of the Enlightenment, human rights, and especially the freedom of faith and its practice, and recognize these also as being essential elements for the authenticity of religion.

As in the Christian community, where there has been a long search to find the correct position of faith in relation to such beliefs—a search that will certainly never be concluded once and for all—so also the Islamic world with its own tradition faces the immense task of finding the appropriate solutions to these problems.

The content of the dialogue between Christians and Muslims will be at this time especially one of meeting each other in this commitment to find the right solutions. We Christians feel ourselves in solidarity with all those who, precisely on the basis of their religious convictions as Muslims, work to oppose violence and for the synergy between faith and reason, between religion and freedom. (Benedict XVI, "Christmas Address to the Roman Curia," *L'Osservatore Romano*, English weekly edition, January 3, 2007, p. 7)

7. Bernard Lewis, deploring the various "blame games" that inhibit reform in the Arab Islamic world, nonetheless writes that "for growing numbers of Middle Easterners, [the blame game] is giving way to a more self-critical approach. The question, 'Who did this to us?' has led only

to neurotic fantasies and conspiracy theories. The other question–'What did we do wrong?'–has led naturally to a second question: 'How do we put it right?' In that question . . . lies the best hope for the future" (Lewis, *What Went Wrong?*, p. 159).

8. Bernard Lewis, "Freedom and Justice in Islam," *Imprimis*, September 2006.

9. On the importance of Holocaust denial in the current unreality that besets too much of the Islamic world, and the necessity of combating it in order to combat jihadism, see Robert Satloff, *Among the Righteous: Lost Stories from the Holocaust's Long Reach into Arab Lands* (New York: PublicAffairs, 2006).

One probe toward something approaching the conversation imagined here may be found in Angel Rabas, Cheryl Benard, Lowell H. Schwartz, and Peter Sickle, *Building Moderate Muslim Networks*, a research paper available from the RAND corporation (see www.rand.org/pubs/monographs.MG574/). The Center for Islamic Pluralism (www.islamicpluralism.org) is another resource for tracking important conversations.

Lesson 7

1. Mark Steyn, *America Alone: The End of the World As We Know It* (Washington, DC: Regnery, 2006), p. 9.

2. Laqueur, *No End to War*, p. 210.

PART TWO: RETHINKING REALISM

Lesson 8

1. Dean Acheson, *Present at the Creation: My Years in the State Department* (New York: Norton, 1987), p. xvii.

2. Charles Frankel, *Morality and U.S. Foreign Policy* (New York: Foreign Policy Association, 1975), p. 52; emphases added.

3. Ajami, *Foreigner's Gift*, p. xix.

Lesson 9

1. Lewis, "Freedom and Justice," p. 5.

2. Michael R. Gordon and General Bernard E. Trainor, *Cobra II: The Inside Story of the Invasion and Occupation of Iraq* (New York: Pantheon Books, 2006), p. 138.

3. Still, General Tommy Franks, the commander of Operation Iraqi Freedom, wanted to try, in one instance. Tired of Syrian interference, Franks memorably said to a colleague, General David McKiernan, "Find out where the knobs are to shut off the oil to Syria–they've been assholes, they continue to be assholes, so I want to turn off their oil" (Gordon and Trainor, *Cobra II*, p. 436).

4. Kaplan, *Imperial Grunts*, p. 185.

5. Ibid., p. 332.

6. Ajami, *Foreigner's Gift*, p. 79.

7. Max Boot, *War Made New: Technology, Warfare, and the Course of History, 1500 to Today* (New York: Gotham Press, 2006), p. 403.

8. David H. Petraeus, "Learning counterinsurgency: Observations from soldiering in Iraq," *Military Review*, January–February 2006, p. 3.

9. For more on the lessons to be taken from this facet of the Iraq experience, see "Lessons Learned about Economic Governance in Wartorn Economies: From the Marshall Plan to the Reconstruction of Iraq," PPC Evaluation Brief #14, February 2006, Bureau for Policy and Program Coordination, U.S. Agency for International Development.

10. Boot, *War Made New*, p. 414.

11. Lewis, *Crisis of Islam*, p. 146.

12. Acheson, *Present at the Creation*, p. 500. NSC-68 was, Acheson wrote in his memoirs, a "difficult pregnancy." There was, for example, enormous resistance to Nitze's and Acheson's work from the then secretary of defense, Louis Johnson. Acheson, seeking to calm the troubled waters, invited Johnson and the Joint Chiefs of Staff to a secret meeting at the Department of State at which Nitze would brief them on what he had written thus far. Johnson, an erratic personality, declared that he did not like meetings for which he had not read the appropriate materials. Walter Isaacson and Evan Thomas then pick up the tale, in *The Wise Men: Six Friends and the World They Made* (New York: Simon and Schuster, 1986):

> Suddenly, [Johnson] lunged forward with a crash of chair legs, pounded his fist on the table, and began accusing Acheson and Nitze of keeping him in the dark and trying to end run him. "I'm not going to be subjected to this indignity!" he stormed. "This is a conspiracy being conducted behind my back in order to subvert my policies! I and the chiefs are leaving now!" He stalked out. The meeting had lasted fourteen minutes. The Department of Defense representative on the committee, Major General James Burns, was so unnerved that he wept. Acheson decided that Johnson was "brain damaged." (p. 500)

Thus was born the strategy that eventually won the Cold War. Which is, I suppose, both a confirmation of the adage that citizens should never see either sausages or policies being made—and a modest comfort in our current circumstances.

Lesson 10

1. Adam Garfinkle, "Culture and Deterrence," Foreign Policy Research Institute E-Notes August 25, 2006, available at http://www.fpri.org.

2. Cited in "Bombing in Paris," *Wall Street Journal*, February 2, 2007.

3. As Bernard Lewis puts it in a 2007 interview with the *Jerusalem Post* ("The Iranians do not expect to be attacked," *Jerusalem Post* online edition, January 31, 2007).

4. Middle East Media Research Institute, "Waiting for the Mahdi: Official Iranian Eschatology Outlined in Public Broadcasting Program in Iran," MEMRI Special Dispatch No. 1436, January 25, 2006, available at http://www.memri.org; R. James Woolsey, testimony before the House Committee on Foreign Affairs, January 11, 2007, available at www.defenddemocracy.org.

5. As the Israeli historian Benny Morris notes, however, this "new Holocaust" would be "quite impersonal," unlike Hitler's Final Solution, where the murderers at least had to look at their victims, however briefly. That impersonality would extend to the millions of Arabs and Muslims killed in any Iranian nuclear attack on Israel—Muslims in Israel proper, and Muslims in the West Bank and Gaza. Still, as Morris writes, "the Iranian leadership sees the destruction of Israel as a supreme divine command, as a herald of the second coming, and Muslims dispatched collaterally [in a nuclear attack on the Jewish state] as so many martyrs in the noble cause." (Benny Mor-

ris, "This Holocaust Will Be Different," *Jerusalem Post*, January 18, 2007).

6. As illustrated, for example, by the following, which is taken from a 2002 op-ed column in Egypt's state-controlled and bestselling newspaper, *Al-Akhbar*:

> The entire matter [of the Holocaust], as many French and British scientists and researchers have proven, is nothing more than a huge Israeli plot aimed at extorting the German government in particular and the European countries in general. But I, personally, and in light of this imaginary tale, complain to Hitler, even saying to him from the bottom of my heart, "If only you had done it, brother, if only it had really happened, so that the world could sigh in relief [without] their evil and sin." (Cited in Matthias Küntzel, "Iran's Obsession with the Jews," *Weekly Standard*, February 19, 2007, p. 19)

7. Küntzel, "Iran's Obsession with the Jews," p. 20.

8. Kenneth R. Timmerman, *Countdown to Crisis: The Coming Nuclear Showdown with Iran* (New York: Crown Forum, 2005), p. 313.

9. Woolsey testimony, January 11, 2007. Former Israeli prime minister Benjamin Netanyahu argued in the late spring of 2007 that the United States and its allies should exploit Iran's economic vulnerabilities; divestment of American pension funds from companies that do business in Iran "could stop Iran dead in its tracks," Netanyahu proposed in "Dealing with Iran," *Wall Street Journal-Europe*, May 28, 2007, p. 15. Norman Podhoretz argues that serious efforts to deny Iran nuclear weapons must include the use

of armed force in "The Case for Bombing Iran," *Commentary*, June 2007, pp. 17–23. The degree to which the International Atomic Energy Agency has consistently underestimated the pace of Iran's developing nuclear capability and the sluggishness of the Security Council suggests that, in any event, it will be a coalition of the willing, not the United Nations, that will affect the needed changes in Iran—one way or another.

10. George P. Shultz, William J. Perry, Henry A. Kissinger, and Sam Nunn, "A World Free of Nuclear Weapons," *Wall Street Journal*, January 4, 2007. Among the specific steps proposed are the following:

Changing the Cold War posture of deployed nuclear weapons to increase warning time and thereby reduce the danger of an accidental or unauthorized use of a nuclear weapon.

Continuing to reduce substantially the size of nuclear forces in all states that possess them.

Eliminating short-range nuclear weapons designed to be forward deployed.

Initiating a bipartisan process with the Senate, including understandings to increase confidence and provide for periodic review, to achieve ratification of the Comprehensive Test Ban Treaty, taking advantage of recent technical advances, and working to secure ratification by other key states.

Providing the highest possible standards of security for all stocks of weapons-usable plutonium and highly enriched uranium everywhere in the world.

Getting control of the uranium enrichment process, combined with the guarantee that uranium for nuclear power reactors could be obtained at a reasonable price, first from the Nuclear Suppliers Group and then from the International Atomic Energy Agency (IAEA) or other controlled international reserves. It will also be necessary to deal with proliferation issues presented by spent fuel from reactors producing electricity.

Halting the production of fissile material for weapons globally; phasing out the use of highly enriched uranium in civil commerce and removing weapons-usable uranium from research facilities around the world and rendering the materials safe.

PART THREE: DESERVING VICTORY

Lesson 11

1. Joseph Ratzinger and Marcello Pera, *Without Roots: The West, Relativism, Christianity, Islam* (New York: Basic Books, 2006), pp. 85–86.

2. On "one-way multiculturalism," see Christopher Hitchens, "Facing the Islamist Menace," *City Journal,* Winter 2007. On "preemptive cringe," see the interview with Bernard Lewis in the *Jerusalem Post,* January 31, 2007.

3. Daniel Henninger, "Western Civ 101: Benedict's Seminar on Fundamentals," *Wall Street Journal,* December 6, 2006.

4. See Kenneth L. Grasso, "Catholicism, Modernity, and the American Proposition," *Journal of Catholic Social Thought* 4:1 (2007), p. 166.

5. Grasso, citing Murray, in "Catholicism, Modernity, and the American Proposition," p. 169.

6. The contrast, noted before, is well drawn by Bernard Lewis in *What Went Wrong?*:

> The idea that any group of persons, any kind of activities, any part of human life is in any sense outside the scope of religious law and jurisdiction is alien to Muslim thought. There is, for example, no distinction between canon law and civil law, between the law of the Church and the law of the state, crucial in Christian history. There is only a single law, the shari'a, accepted by Muslims as of divine origin and regulating all aspects of human life: civil, commercial, criminal, constitutional, as well as matters more specifically concerned with religion in the limited, Christian sense of that word. (p. 100)

7. Lewis, *Muslim Discovery of Europe*, p. 296.

8. Bernard Lewis, 2007 Irving Kristol Lecture, available at www.aei.org/include/pub print.asp?pubID-25815.

9. Cited in Sandro Magister, "The Lecture in Regensburg Continues to Weigh on the Islamic Question," at www.chiesa.espressonline.it, December 4, 2006.

Lesson 12

1. Melanie Phillips, *Londonistan* (New York: Encounter Books, 2006), p. ix. It is instructive, if depressing, to reflect on the fact that Ms. Phillips's book was rejected by several mainstream UK publishers, in yet another demonstration of self-imposed dhimmitude.

2. Daniel Johnson, "Terror & Denial," *Commentary*, July–August 2006. Johnson notes that Sir Iqbal was knighted at the same time as Jonathan Sacks, chief rabbi of Great Britain, "evidently for reasons of multicultural balance–though there is no intellectual or moral comparison between Sacks, one of Britain's most respected religious leaders, and Sacranie, who rose to prominence by

supporting Ayatollah Khomeini's fatwa against Salman Rushdie. Though he is the government's chief Muslim interlocutor, Sacranie has an avowedly anti-Zionist and anti-Semitic agenda: he justifies Hamas suicide bombings, boycotts Holocaust commemorations, and harasses pro-Israel politicians. When his equivocal attitude toward terrorism was exposed by a BBC documentary [in 2005], Sacranie accused his critics of being part of a Zionist conspiracy."

3. Cited in Mark Steyn, "The Moderate Mosque," *Chicago Sun-Times*, February 21, 2007.

4. *Charlie Hebdo*'s editor, Philippe Val, discusses the kowtowing of the French government, which put him in grave legal jeopardy, in "Modern Blasphemy," *Wall Street Journal*, March 21, 2007. Alas, Mr. Val himself misses a crucial point when he writes that "when religion leaves the private sphere it becomes an ideology like any other, and must accept to be criticized with the same virulence as any other ideology." However much one objects to the prosecution of Mr. Val on bogus racism charges, this formulation is another crude expression of *laïcité*, which is itself an ideology. Christianity, for example, has an inherently public character, and it does not "become an ideology" when it "leaves the private sphere." The answer to false charges of "racism" and Islamist pressures cannot be a public arena scoured of religiously informed argument.

5. Stephen Dinan and Jerry Seper, "NFL Rejects Border Patrol Ad," *Washington Times*, February 14, 2007. The NFL tried to excuse itself by suggesting that the ad's further reference to stopping drugs and illegal aliens at the border was "controversial," given the then-heated

debate on immigration reform policy. One might also, of course, wonder at the government's prudence in trying to spend taxpayer money in this priciest of advertising venues.

For an intriguing look at Islamist recruitment in the United States, see Daveed Gartenstein-Ross, *My Year Inside Radical Islam* (New York: Tarcher, 2007).

Lesson 13

1. Bernard Lewis suggests an interesting analogy: "Imagine that the Ku Klux Klan or some similar group obtains total control of the state of Texas, of its oil and therefore of its oil revenues, and having done so, uses this money to establish a network of well-endowed schools and colleges all over Christendom, peddling their peculiar brand of Christianity." But Lewis immediately goes on to note that "this parallel is somewhat less dire than the reality, since most Christian countries have functioning public schools systems of their own." In any event, Lewis sums up the Wahhabi/Saudi/oil nexus in these terms: "The custodianship of the holy places and the revenues of oil have given worldwide impact to what would otherwise have been an extremist fringe in a marginal country" (*Crisis of Islam*, p. 111).

2. One such attempt at defining a new, bipartisan national energy strategy may be found in "Ending the Energy Stalemate," the report of the National Commission on Energy Policy, available at www.energycommission.org.

3. See R. James Woolsey, testimony before the U.S. Senate Committee on Energy and Natural Resources, March 7, 2006, available at http://energy.senate.gov/public/.

4. Ibid.

5. R. James Woolsey, "Gentlemen, Start Your Plug-Ins," *Wall Street Journal*, December 30, 2006.

6. David Sandalow, "Ending Oil Dependence," January 22, 2007, pp. 19–20, available as download from Brookings Institution website, http://www.brook.edu/default.htm.

7. Ibid., p. 14.

8. Ibid., p. 18.

Lesson 14

1. Mary Eberstadt, "The Scapegoats Among Us," *Policy Review* 140 (December 2006–January 2007).

2. Mark Steyn, for example, makes an important point while tormenting the Rt. Rev. Katherine Jeffords Schori, the first woman to be Presiding Bishop of the Episcopal Church, USA:

> Bishop Kate gave an interview to the *New York Times* revealing what passes for orthodoxy in this most flexible of faiths. She was asked a simple enough question: "How many members of the Episcopal Church are there?" "About 2.2 million," replied the presiding bishop. "It used to be larger percentage-wise, but Episcopalians tend to be better educated and tend to reproduce at lower rates than other denominations."
>
> This was a bit of a jaw-dropper even for a *New York Times* hackette, so, with vague memories of God saying something about going forth and multiplying floating around in the back of her head, a bewildered Deborah Solomon said: "Episcopalians aren't interested in replenish-

ing their ranks by having children?" "No," agreed Bishop
Kate. "It's probably the opposite. We encourage people to
pay attention to the stewardship of the earth and not use
more than their portion."

...Here's the question for Bishop Kate: if Fatma
An-Najar [a 64-year-old Palestinian homicide-bomber/
grandmother] has 41 grandchildren and a responsible 'bet-
ter-educated' Episcopalian has one or two, into whose
hands are we delivering the "stewardship of the earth?" If
your crowd isn't around in any numbers, how much influence can they have in shaping the future? ("Quartet of Ladies
Shows Where We're Heading," *Chicago Sun-Times*, November 26, 2006)

3. "Statement on Baghdad Museum," American
Schools of Oriental Research, April 16, 2003, http://www.
aser.org/policy2.htm.

4. Gerard Baker, "Oh George, What Will We Do When
You're Gone?" *The Times*, March 2, 2007.

5. Cited in Eberstadt, "The Scapegoats Among Us."
Eberstadt freely concedes the necessity of law enforcement
and rational immigration policies. But she is also devastating in her critique of the Unhinged Right's target misiden-
tification:

The undocumented Mexicans, like the furor they have at-
tracted out of all proportion to the actual problems they
pose, are serving a larger communal purpose [i.e., denial of
the real threat, which is jihadism]...[C]onsider...what a
world designed along contemporary anti-immigration principles might resemble. As they often emphasize, the theo-
rists overwhelmingly concerned with Hispanics do not

oppose all immigration. [Patrick] Buchanan, for one, concludes *State of Emergency* with a specific list of traits for would-be immigrants to whom he would rather give preference: those who speak English, who can contribute significantly to American society, who have an education, who come from countries with a history of assimilation in America, who will not become public charges, and who wish to become Americans.

Yet using that same list, one can see that four out of six conditions were fulfilled by architecture graduate student Mohammad Atta, affluent private school graduate Ziad Jarrah, military scholarship–winning Marwan al-Shehhi, and for that matter most of the other 9/11 hijackers and other al-Qaeda terrorists caught since then. Add that anyone English-speaking and determined enough could presumably charm an INS officer into believing that they wish to become Americans, and it turns out that such men could have fulfilled not four but five of the six conditions. Now bear in mind that several could have claimed ties to a white-collar profession–airplane piloting–and we have here a nearly model list of potentially attractive immigrants. Is it a problem that Buchanan's list theoretically inclines toward men like these and against the grape-picking, toilet-cleaning Mexicans whose idea of Wal-Mart is a gift card rather than a car bomb? Common sense says that it is.

6. "Peanuts for Petraeus," *Wall Street Journal*, March 17, 2007.

7. Cited in J. R. Dunn, "Breaking the Hold of Hegemonist Doctrine," January 5, 2007, at www.realclearpolitics.com.

8. Cited in Kathy Kiely and Ken Dilanian, "Democrats Draw Up Iraq Deadlines," *USA Today*, March 9, 2007.

9. David Frum described both in an August 2006 op-ed essay:

> It's possible . . . to take four or five basic pieces of information about somebody (such as name, address, phone number, date of birth) and match them against the commercial databases used by mortgage companies and credit card issuers to arrive at a surprisingly sophisticated terrorist risk profile of each passenger.
>
> If, for example, you are a 38-year-old-woman, married and the mother of three, who has lived at the same address for three years, has traveled to Barbados with her three children for Christmas for the past three years and is about to go again: Well, you present a fairly low risk. Airline security might still ask you to walk through a metal detector just to be on the safe side, but it should not waste too much time on you beyond that.
>
> Another approach: Perhaps if you fly often from New York to London, you might be willing to volunteer a whole mass of information to British Airways in return for a "safe traveler" card that will allow you to walk on the plane with minimum fuss. Your name might be Omar Abdullah, but if they know you are 57 years old, director of the Middle East collection at the Metropolitan Museum, own an apartment in Manhattan and a brokerage account at Merrill Lynch, carry a Visa card with a $50,000 limit, fly to London six times a year with tickets paid for by the museum, and so on and so on . . . well, they can pretty well confidently let you on the plane with minimal formalities.

Please notice that neither program . . . would make any use of information about ethnicity or religion. They would not in any sense of the term be "racial profiling." Please note as well that both would use only information that the individual himself had voluntarily provided either directly to the airline or to other commercial entities–no government coercion would be involved.

Yet both these approaches have been effectively banned in the United States . . . Why? Congress and the TSA [Transportation Security Administration] have surrendered to pressure from advocacy groups who fear that if we concentrate enforcement resources where they will do the most good, we will end up concentrating them upon unattached Muslim men. Very few Muslims are Islamic terrorists, but all Islamic terrorists are Muslims. Our pre-screening process may be ethnically neutral, but the results will not be.

But isn't that precisely the way security is supposed to work? ("Flying Blind," *National Post,* August 12, 2006)

10. Michael Fumento notes that "the only green beret ever awarded to a woman came from a judge. According to retired Special Forces officer Lt. Col. William E. Bailey, Cpt. Kathleen Wilder attended all three phases of Special Forces training in the summer of 1980, but during the final week 'she and two male students were caught caching their rucksacks.' That is, she and her compatriots were not carrying the rucksacks as required by the instructors, but hiding them to pick up at a later time and date in what is referred to as a Mission Support Site. All three were dropped from the course, ostensibly for cheating.' The men

accepted the outcome, Bailey has written, but Wilder got a lawyer who argued she was a victim of sex discrimination. The court agreed, ordering that she receive a course completion certificate. She never spent a day in an actual Special Forces unit, but she continues to play off her reputation as 'the nation's only female Green Beret' " ("The Democrats' Special Forces Fetish," *Weekly Standard*, March 5, 2007, p. 23).

11. David B. Rivkin, Jr., and Lee A. Casey, "Lawfare," *Wall Street Journal*, February 23, 2007.

12. Ibid.

13. See United States District Court for the Eastern District of Michigan, Southern Division, *American Civil Liberties Union et alia v. National Security Agency et alia*, August 17, 2006.

Lesson 15

1. See, for example, Nick Cohen, "An Upside-Down World," *Wall Street Journal*, January 25, 2007; Bret Stephens, "Islamosocialism," *Wall Street Journal*, March 18, 2007.

2. On this point, see Joshua Muravchik, "Urgent: Operation Comeback," *Foreign Policy*, November–December 2006.

3. Robert R. Reilly, "Britney vs. the Terrorists," *Washington Post*, February 9, 2007.

4. Ibid.

On the incapacities of Al-Hurra, intended as an "answer" to Al-Jazeera, see Joel Mowbrayt, "Mad TV," *Wall Street Journal*, May 1, 2007, p. A21.

5. Middle East Media Research Institute, Islamist Websites Monitor Project, Nos. 52–55 (MEMRI Special Dis-

patches 1434–35, 1437, 1439), January 23–26, 2007, http://www.memri.org/iwmp.html.

6. Lewis interview, *Jerusalem Post*, January 31, 2007.

7. Michael Gerson, "The Nation May Be Tired, but History Doesn't Care," *Newsweek*, August 21–28, 2006.

8. Dunn, "Breaking the Hold of Hegemonist Doctrine."

9. David Gelernter, "Please Say This . . . ," *Weekly Standard*, January 22, 2007.

GEORGE WEIGEL, Distinguished Senior Fellow of Washington's Ethics and Public Policy Center, is a Catholic theologian and one of America's foremost commentators on issues of religion and public life. A *Newsweek* contributor and Vatican analyst for NBC News, Weigel is the author of fifteen books, including the *New York Times* bestseller *Witness to Hope: The Biography of Pope John Paul II*. His work has been translated into more than a dozen languages.